My Perfect Storm

A Story To Be Told
A 50-Year Journey
from Chaos To Calm

Scott Brearley

First published by Ultimate World Publishing 2024
Copyright © 2024 Scott Brearley

ISBN

Paperback: 978-1-923123-74-8
Ebook: 978-1-923123-75-5

Scott Brearley has asserted his rights under the Copyright, Designs and Patents Act 1988 to be identified as the author of this work. The information in this book is based on the author's experiences and opinions. The publisher specifically disclaims responsibility for any adverse consequences which may result from use of the information contained herein. Permission to use information has been sought by the author. Any breaches will be rectified in further editions of the book.

All rights reserved. No part of this publication may be reproduced, stored in or introduced into a retrieval system, or transmitted in any form, or by any means (electronic, mechanical, photocopying, recording or otherwise) without the prior written permission of the author. Any person who does any unauthorized act in relation to this publication may be liable to criminal prosecution and civil claims for damages. Enquiries should be made through the publisher.

Cover design: Ultimate World Publishing
Layout and typesetting: Ultimate World Publishing
Editor: Rebecca Low

Ultimate World Publishing
Diamond Creek,
Victoria Australia 3089
www.writeabook.com.au

Testimonials

Forty-two years ago I met Scott at an AA meeting that was being held at an Ontario Correctional Facility. After I spoke at this meeting, I met Scott and saw him as the cute little boy who may have come to the meeting for cigarettes and coffee but underneath I saw a cocky, angry man who really didn't give a damn. As I watched him grow into a man, I saw so much more in Scott. There was love, kindness, and joy. He always had determination and an amazing work ethic. Scott enhanced my life and gave me someone to love, talk to, to help guide and brought meaning in my life. I am so proud that he calls me his mother and I know he will bring truth, honour, respect, dignity, accountability and reliability to those he loves. It is a pure joy to see the love and respect that Scott and his wife Lisa have for each other. I love Scott dearly and I am proud to call him my son. All the best to my son Scott.

AKA - Mom, Phyllis Muller

Scott has spent the majority of his life trying to run from his past; building up walls and living in solitude. When I connected with Scott about five years ago, his hurt was disguised behind a tough-guy persona. Despite the hardships Scott faced throughout his childhood, especially with his family, he was full of unconditional love, forgiveness, and courage. Over the past couple of years, I have witnessed Scott be reborn. I have seen a man full of hurt, anger, and resentment, peel off the tough-guy mask and show the world who he truly is. Scott has transformed from the man who pulled himself out of a hole to the man who will stretch out his hand to help others out of theirs.

Niece, Tara Brearley

As time went on, things were getting worse and worse for me and my depression grew to the point that sucking on the barrel of a gun was a very good idea in my mind. At this time Scott came to me and asked me if I would be willing to be coached by him. I did give it some serious thought, and since I liked the changes I've seen in him, I said 'yes'. This was definitely one of my better decisions I've made in quite some time. Did the changes within me happen overnight? No. However, while receiving Scott's support, I've been able to come out from under a heavy bolder of major depression and start living again. I am truly happy now and I love to watch my grandchildren grow and laugh. Thanks Scott for all your help.

Friend, Mark Hartnett

I have known Scott for about 20 years. Scott was there for me at one of my lowest and most difficult times when he and his wife, at the time, jumped on a plane to Mexico and helped me out. That is when I truly realized what an amazing, empathetic person he was. I have watched Scott go through difficulties with relationships, family and health issues. At times I was afraid he would not make it to the other side and would never believe in his self-worth and I would lose him to suicide. Since Scott began his forward walking journey the change has been AMAZING!!! He now believes in himself and the value he has to offer others. He has found joy in all aspects of his life and now values self and others. He has found his beautiful wife Lisa and they have truly enriched each other's lives. I like to think of Scott as my little brother and I am forever grateful to have him in my life.

Friend, Colleen Mclennan

There are very few times in your life when you meet someone with a unique combination of humility, courage, strength, integrity, openness and vulnerability, while having lived experiences that even half the volume, would take most people out of commission. Scott is one of those rare individuals. From the moment I met him I knew he was different and I also knew he would do whatever it took, for as long as it took to get to the goals he had for himself and later Lisa once they had become a couple. With heart, dedication and true grit, he persevered and never gave up. He faced opportunity and adversity equally, learning to enjoy the gifts from both. Watching Scott grow & heal to where he is now has been an honor and a privilege and seeing how he continues to use his life to gift others in any way he can, gives hope in a world where so many only focus on themselves. I can truly and honestly say my life is richer for having met Scott and I am truly excited for him on this next chapter in his life and all those that will be lucky enough to share in his gifts.

Founder, Katalyst Integrated Trauma Treatment, Kimberly Davidson

Dedication

This book is dedicated to you—the reader. I know you've struggled at some point in your life, and my book is here to show you that CHANGE IS POSSIBLE. No matter what.

Through my journey of addiction, 12-step programs, therapists, and personal development work, I've come to see it's all about your choices and the decisions we make. I know that through my story, you'll see that too.

Were these choices easy for me? HELL NO, however, they were my FORWARD WALKING CHOICES and, sometimes, my backward walking choices. My journey of failures, challenges, and successes has forged the more compassionate and loving man I am today.

Like me, you may have doubted yourself and your worth. You may have had many times in life when you felt like you didn't fit in and life wasn't worth living. You may have even contemplated or attempted to end it all. I'm here to say that your life is worth it. You're worth it. I'm worth it, too.

Contents

Testimonials — iii
Dedication — vii
Introduction — 1
Preface — 5
CHAPTER 1: My Turbulent, Unpredictable Beginnings — 7
CHAPTER 2: Glimpses of Calm in the Shit Storm — 19
CHAPTER 3: Intense, Turbulent Fronts — 29
CHAPTER 4: Growing Intensity — 37
CHAPTER 5: Misleading Glimpses of Escape in a Destructive Storm — 47
CHAPTER 6: Some Warmth — 55
CHAPTER 7: A Positive Glimpse Amongst the Damage — 69
CHAPTER 8: What a Fool to Think I Could Escape the Storm — 79
CHAPTER 9: Break Free From the Severe Damage — 91
CHAPTER 10: The High Waters Seemed to Be Falling — 99
CHAPTER 11: The Fuckin' Rising Temperatures Again — 115
CHAPTER 12: Some Clearing in the Shit Storm — 133
CHAPTER 13: Major Forces of Disruption — 141
CHAPTER 14: Comfort from the Storm? — 155
CHAPTER 15: Life with Sunnier Days — 165
CHAPTER 16: More Calm and Radiance — 181
CHAPTER 17: Embracing the Warmth of the Sun, the Wind in My Hair, and the Blue Skies — 195
Three Offers With Calls To Action — 203
Speaker Bio — 205

Introduction

Hello, my name is Scott Allen Brearley.

I'm a 56-year-old man and I've been around the 12-step programs since I was 15. That got me to a certain point, and then I was lost. I kept doing the same thing over and over. In the end, I needed to walk away to grow.

I'm a man who was raised in a home that bred addiction and where violence was prominent. I never knew what safe was when I was at home and never knew who to trust. I know my story is the same as many other people. There was always booze around. Mom and dad fought about everything.

I had tried sipping drinks and got really drunk at my sister's wedding when I was 12. It was around the same time that I started smoking pot. It was like my body craved it. At this early age, my addiction was off and running.

I stole money from the beginning to get more drugs. I was called a little puke by my mom and was told I would never amount to anything. I got into fights all the time.

I thought my life was normal and thought everyone did it. By the time I was 15, I drank and smoked weed daily, always looking for the next high.

My Perfect Storm

I was out of control, on a suicide mission from the first time I got high.

My whole life, I've always chased people to be in my life like I was never good enough or could never measure up, no matter how long I had been clean.

I was in and out of jail, exactly where my family thought I should be. I fit in there, or so I thought.

Getting sober was difficult at first. I was going to 12-step meetings, surrounded by people doing the same thing. I felt like I fit in for the first time in my life.

I look back and see it was just a semi-safe place to work on changing my life. The 12-step programs are great, to a point. I wouldn't be where I am today if I hadn't spent years going to them. However, for me, I needed more therapy.

Today, my opinion is a little different. After years of being in and out of 12-step meetings, I see that there are a lot of great people in A.A. and N.A.; however, there are also a lot of sick people, so I have to be careful. I don't think it's as black and white as laid out in the literature.

There's lots of gossip, and I found that people never let you change. We can become as stuck there as in active addiction. I went back and tried the same thing over and over, expecting different results. That sounds a little like an addiction. Or the definition of insanity.

I got to a point where I was sicker in recovery than when I was loaded 24/7. I spent years like this with it so ingrained in me that I was doomed to jail or death if I left the 12-step world. Well, at many points, I had welcomed death. I pushed everyone out of my life.

Introduction

Alone and scared with some new medical problems from not looking after myself, I sought out a different direction. I went to the Personal Success Institute (PSI) for a three-day weekend course that teaches you how to show up for life.

Over the years, I had worked on a lot of what they showed me that weekend, which helped me grow. On the last day of the course, they attempted to up-sell all of us for their next course. I was mad and thought, *how dare they?* I went out to my Harley to ride home, and I thought to myself, *I want to die. Why was I so unwilling to spend money on my mental health?* I went back in and signed up for the next course.

Around the same time, I sought out a professional to help with all the trauma I had in my life. From there, I learned how to stop living life from a victim's stance. I met Kimberly Davidson, an amazing lady at Katalyst Integrated Trauma Treatment. She was a pivotal part of a big shift in my life.

So, I invite you to come on my journey with me. Read my book and tell me what you think. I hope my turbulent past and major life changes help you in your journey to find recovery like I have today. My beliefs have changed drastically where addiction and alcoholism are concerned.

Thank you,

Scott Allen Brearley

Preface

So, it begins.

I would have laughed if you told me I was going to write a book at the age of 55. I would have put myself down and made excuses. I've had a difficult life.

I'm a 55-year-old man. I've struggled all my life with injuries, addiction, and loneliness. I've had feelings of stupidity and struggled for happiness or purpose. In my life, I've always slipped through the cracks.

For many years, people have told me that they see a leader in me and that I will do great things in life.

But then I would stumble again. And again. And again.

As I grew and changed, self-doubt was always on my ass.

I grew up in Burlington, Ontario, Canada. I'm the son of Barbara Jean Bronson (Brearley) and Ronald Earl Brearley.

I was the youngest of five children. Gary was the oldest, and Lorie was born about a year later. Doug came along about two years after Lorie, and within another year, Ted was born.

My Perfect Storm

Then, five years later, I was the last Brearley child. My lasting impression of being born as a boy was that my mom wanted me to be a girl, and she never let me forget it.

What I remember about my childhood is that I really didn't have one. At least not one where children feel they can really just be children. No worries. Carefree. My home was full of violence and tension.

Because of my trauma-filled life and a major accident at the age of seven, my memory of exact dates is very unclear. All I remember is that I had a sense of survival in my house and that I didn't really feel loved.

I know that my home was not a place where love really existed. My home was a place where I never found true support or help.

This book is about how I remember both the big and minor events in my life. For you, my story may feel broken and disjointed, and for me, my life *was* broken and disjointed.

In writing this book, I have worked through many tough memories, ones that haunt and trouble me. There are many memories that make me doubt why I'm even worthy to be alive.

This is a recount of my life. A journey filled with anger and mistrust and, later, a life that I never even thought was possible for a man like me. A life of liberty and love; however, the memories still linger and have so strongly imprinted on my soul that the struggle is always just a moment away.

CHAPTER 1

My Turbulent, Unpredictable Beginnings

I'm going to kill that little son of a bitch...

Our family did attempt to do some typical family things. However, the part that I remember is that dad was always drinking and even had his own beer fridge. We did a lot of camping over the years when I was young, and there were some great feelings around those camping adventures that we went on.

My Perfect Storm

On one of our camping trips, we were camping in Kill Bear Park. Since our site was on the beach, I wandered back to our tent trailer for a nap without telling anyone. I was sound asleep until dad's voice startled me awake. He was yelling, "I'm going to kill that little son of a bitch when I get my hands on him."

I remember laying there terrified, not sure what to do. If I said anything, I knew I would get a beating. So, I hid. I didn't move.

One of my older brothers came in and found me there. To my surprise, I didn't get a beating. There was no physical punishment this time, but the verbal threat was the all-consuming punishment that I received that day.

You're no good

I have very few memories of happy times in my life.

When I was young, I had two bunny rabbits named Casey and Finnegan, which you may know from the Canadian T.V. show *Mister Dress Up*. I really liked those bunnies.

I had accidentally left the rabbit's cage door open, and they ran away. I was heartbroken. They were something I loved, and I think they kind of loved me back. I remember being scolded during dinner by the whole family, as they said, "You need to be more responsible."

In the later years, I found out that it was actually my parents who gave my rabbits away without telling me, and then they actually left the door open to make it look like I did it. And, of course, I was easily blamed.

My Turbulent, Unpredictable Beginnings

I felt like I was given mixed messages growing up. I love you, but you're no good. I never felt safe with my family. Not feeling safe did a lot of damage to me. Reflecting back, my home was not a home as I felt like I was in a constant state of fear. Fear of violence and the lack of unconditional love really haunted me.

Drowning

One memory that puts a smile on my face is how I loved Johnny Cash.

I remember a Christmas when I got a little guitar and pretended I was Johnny Cash. That was a good memory.

I do remember we had a big, red station wagon. It was fun when we went camping, as my parents made a bed in the back for me to sleep in for the drive up to Kill Bear Park.

My grandfather, of whom I have a few distinct memories, had a speed boat that we could take out to go water skiing. I don't remember ever trying water skiing myself, but I remember it was fun watching some older siblings and family members do it.

This one time, when we were on the speedboat, my mom fell overboard. That was a very intense moment for me. She panicked because she thought she was going to drown, as she couldn't swim, but my Aunt Cathy told her that she was on a sandbar and could stand up.

These are just some of the damaging memories that have really stuck with me over the years. Watching my family joke about scary things like drowning or my dad yelling out loud that he was going to kill me.

Only during the later years of my life did I really begin to realize the negative impact it had on me and my trust in others.

I can do this

When I was about four or five years old, I was left at home with my siblings while my mom had gone shopping at the Loblaws grocery store. I was scared in the house, so I left on my own and walked to the store. I knew I could find my way, but it was longer than I thought. When I got there, my mom was very angry that I walked all by myself.

I'm different

When I started kindergarten, my mom got her first job. She started working in the kitchen of an old age home. Because she was busy working, I had to go to a stranger's house after school. A mother of a kid from my kindergarten class looked after me.

The rules there were way different than at my house, and I didn't want to go. This wasn't fair. This was the first time I felt different than my siblings. They never had to experience being looked after by someone else.

Did not say goodbye
We would go to church on Sunday, with everyone grumbling about not wanting to go but mom made us. She was pretty involved with the church.

I didn't like church except for Easter when we would cook pancakes. We were allowed to eat as much as we wanted. That was a fun memory.

My Turbulent, Unpredictable Beginnings

Mom met some people from the church who had a sailboat. We would go out with them a few times a month. It was a lot of fun.

The big holidays or long weekends were a big thing in our family. We would have other family come to our house, or we would go to their house to have some fun together. In later years, the family get-togethers were called the Brearley or Bronson Brawls.

My aunt Cathy was always extra nice. She would come and get me and take me places to have fun. Aunt Cathy looked after a girl named Tracy, who was my age.

I remember going downhill skiing, and I made the front page of the *Kitchener Harold*, the local newspaper. I got dragged by the T-bar, holding on for dear life, not willing to let go. That's the picture I've included on the front of this book.

Grandpa Bill

As I said before, I do remember having some happy times in my life when I was young. My grandparents, Bill and Amy Bronson, had an in-ground pool.

It was fun going to their house. My grandfather loved family and getting together. Grandpa Bill would always be throwing someone in the pool. They had this ski belt that I would wear. However, if I got turned upside down, I couldn't right myself up.

One day, Grandpa was bent over, doing something in the pool before he was off to work, and at that time, he was wearing a suit for work. At last, I saw my chance to have a little fun with my grandpa like he often did with me. I pushed him into the pool. He was angry. I knew I was going to get it. I ran. He chased me and was yelling. I was scared and confused because he threw everyone else in the pool.

My grandmother came to my rescue. She got between my grandfather and me and protected me from him.

These types of incidents were all very confusing to my understanding of what love really was. They all seemed to compound in me, and for some reason, the negative memories far outweighed the positive ones. They helped create the person I thought I was and how I was to show up in this life.

Grammy

When I was six, my grandmother (Grammy) had become ill all of a sudden. I remember being in the hallway at the hospital, left all alone. I didn't know what was going on. I was just so confused. No one was telling me anything.

My parents decided not to let me see my grandmother. I don't know whether they did it out of concern for me and protecting me from seeing my grandmother dying or they just didn't care. However, I remember thinking this was just not fair. My grandmother passed away. I think this is when things started to really go south. Her passing rocked the family.

I was really starting to feel like a nobody. I remember during one of our dinners, I raised my voice to be heard, and almost in unison, everyone said, "Shut up."

Being spanked was a big form of punishment, mostly from my dad. My brothers fought all the time. Ted would tease and bully me and call me stupid. Being the youngest in the family, I felt like all I was doing was surviving.

The accident

When I was seven, I played with the kids who lived behind us. One of the kids was a girl. I remember teasing her by stealing her skipping rope. She went to tell her mom. I dropped the rope and ran into a car as I was running across the street. I was dragged 40 yards. I sustained multiple fractures on both legs, my left arm was broken, my lung had collapsed, and I had a fractured skull. The doctors told my parents to start making arrangements for me as I may not make it.

When this accident happened, my grandfather had just gotten remarried to Bernice, and he was on his honeymoon. Things were not looking good for me, and it was decided not to tell my grandfather till he got home from his honeymoon.

Bernice and Grandpa came to the hospital from the airport. I was told he yelled, "Get up and at 'em, boy." He yelled at me that this was not my time to die. Apparently, this is when I had my turnaround and started to improve.

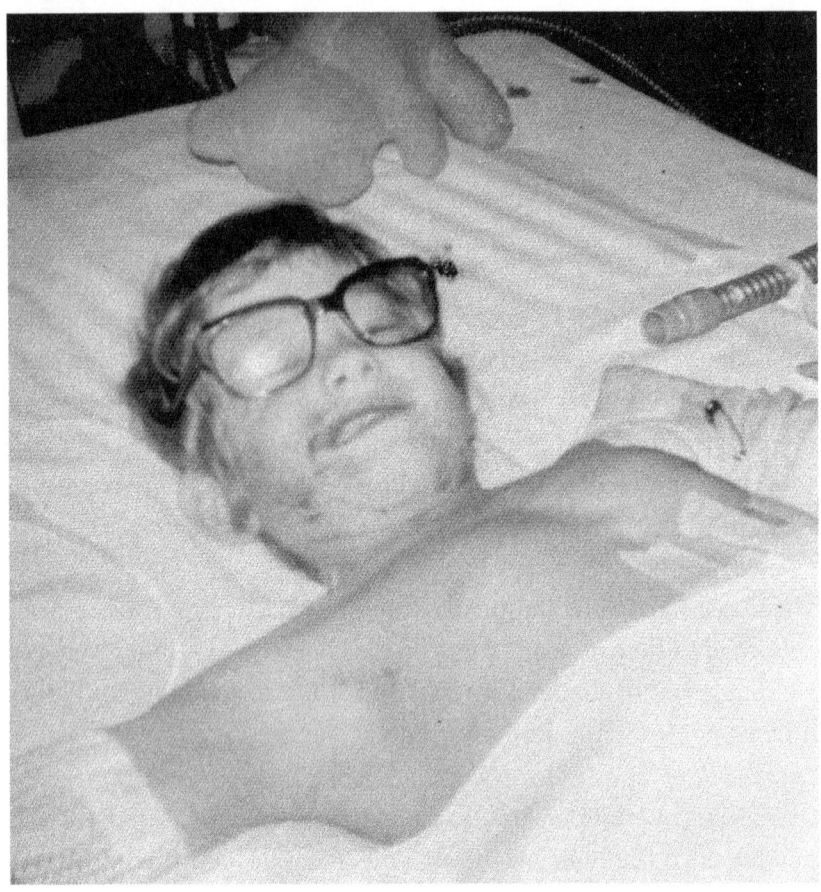

Scott in the hospital at age 7
with his Grandfather's glasses on.

Oozing and ice cream

I remember being in the emergency department at the hospital. I was in traction with my legs in the air with those rubber tensor bandages wrapped around a steel pole, so I wasn't able to move.

My Turbulent, Unpredictable Beginnings

There were tubes in my right arm and ooze coming out from the incision made during my lung surgery.

There was a male nurse. I remember thinking, *a male nurse, that's funny.* I thought only women were nurses. He brought me ice cream.

After this, my memory is a little hazy. I do remember lots of pain and the full cast from my hips to my toes.

The stench and whatever oozed from my lungs was nasty. I would wipe it with Kleenex. The nurses would give me hell, saying it would get infected if I kept it up.

At some point, I was able to go home, and the Red Cross loaned us a hospital bed that I could keep in my bedroom.

I was now in the newspaper again for another thing that, however you looked at it, was drawing attention to my mistakes.

Bedridden at home

My dad, as the maintenance man at Butler Manufacturing, came home one day with a TV from the people who worked with him. I guess they all chipped in and thought it would be helpful since I had to stay in bed to recover.

A girl from school and her little sister came over to see me. They wanted to sign my cast, so the little sister pulled the blanket down and exposed my privates to them. I was so embarrassed. I had a crush on the girl, and now she saw me naked.

My Perfect Storm

At some point, I had gained some of my strength back. My brother Ted carried me downstairs. He was being nice, I guess, to get me out of my bedroom since I was still stuck in the cast.

My mom came home from work and went to see me in my room and freaked out because I wasn't there. She yelled and was frantically looking for me even though I was just downstairs watching T.V.

At the time, I remember being excited about being out of my room. I thought my mom should be happy for me because I was getting better. From the work I have done over the past few years, I realize that it was times like this when these overreactions contributed to my path of destruction. I felt like I wasn't good enough or I was making poor choices.

Starting to heal
The girl that drove the car I ran into was only 16 and had just gotten her licence. Her family felt bad for me, so when they later went on a trip to Disneyland, they brought me back lots of cool things. Some Mickey Mouse stuff and a fun kaleidoscope.

My Turbulent, Unpredictable Beginnings

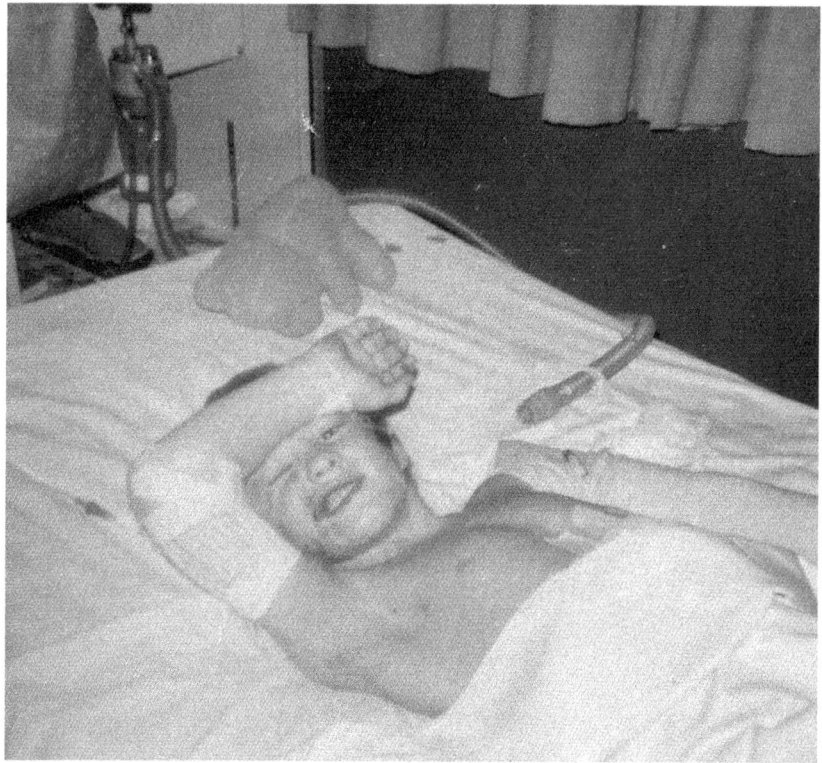

Scott smiling while in the hospital after his major accident.

After some time at home with the cast from my waist down, it was time to go back to the hospital to have the cast removed, which hurt a lot. My legs were all covered in cotton. They kept me for a while. I had to have lots of baths to get all the cotton off my legs. I was embarrassed that the nurses had seen me naked.

I thought I would be able to walk right away, but I was bedridden in the hospital and needed therapy to learn how to walk again. I remember a boy who kept jumping all over my bed and over my sore legs in the kids' playroom. It was painful, and I can't remember what was done about it; I just remember him doing lots of jumping on me.

My Perfect Storm

The therapist started me on crutches. When my parents came to visit, I was in the hallway with the nurse, practicing walking. I was proud I was on my feet again, even if I was walking with crutches. I thought I could show my parents how strong I was and lifted both crutches off the ground, and bam—I was on the floor. I was so embarrassed. My stupid button was pressed again.

CHAPTER 2

Glimpses of Calm in the Shit Storm

School

Shortly after learning how to use the crutches, I got to go home. I still couldn't walk very well, but by this time, it was winter, and the school wanted me to attend, as I had missed a lot. So, the teachers came to my house and pulled me through the snow to school on a sled.

My Perfect Storm

Scott coming home after his cast was removed
from his major car accident at age 7.

I had a wheelchair at school. They thought it would be best for me to move up a grade to stay with my friends.

At home, I learned how to walk slowly. I would go from door frame to door frame to the couch to the counter.

Glimpses of Calm in the Shit Storm

Summer finally came

My brother, Gary, was working for some guy named Ken Kelly, who had a son, Mathew, who was younger than me. Gary took me to play with him all the time. I was able to walk at this point, but I had weak legs.

They got me a trike to ride, as I could no longer ride a two-wheeler. I didn't have the strength in my legs. I was embarrassed; not only did I have to play with younger kids, but now I was on a trike.

I do remember going to Matthew's house, where the kids could do whatever they wanted. There was no yelling, just having fun. We could go on the roof of their house and play, and nothing was said.

Lady, our family dog, would go with us. When they fed their dog, King, he would stand and watch Lady eat till she had her fill, and then King would eat.

Gary's boss had a hockey school. He tried talking to my mom into letting me skate. She wouldn't let me, which I wasn't happy about. I guess my mom was scared I would get hurt again.

Tim, Tom, and Len

When school started up again, they decided to make me do grade three again. Grade three is where I met Tim, Tom, and Len.

I started getting in trouble for farting in class and acting out. I would be sent to stand in the hallway alot.

I started teasing the 'special' kids and was getting into fights.

I felt like I didn't fit in.

The school started making me go to special education classes. The teacher there was great, and he would give us Lifesaver candies all the time.

The many accidents

Gary took me to Bronte Creek, and I jumped off the concrete pillars into the river on the side that was shallow. I cut my foot open and had to get stitches. I think this was the first time I went to the hospital for stitches.

After that, I spent a lot of time in and out of the hospital for stitches. At one point, they called the cops on my dad to question him about my injuries and see if it was from abuse at home or not. Back then, this wasn't done very much. People minded their own affairs.

At home, there was lots of drinking and fighting or arguing. It seemed like everything revolved around drinking when the families got together. Almost all my aunts and uncles drank.

Uncle Joe

My dad's brother, Uncle Joe, moved back from Scotland, as he was living there for some time. I had never met Uncle Joe.

Uncle Joe was a lot of fun. He was cool, a little bit of a rebel, which I liked. Uncle Joe had met Sandra in Scotland, and she came later to Canada and, of course, had soon become my aunt. I liked Aunt Sandra. It was fun to tease her. She spoke funny (that Scottish accent) and was almost as small as me! She actually wore some of my shoes and clothes when she first got to Canada.

We had lots of family time with Uncle Joe and Aunt Sandra. Aunt Sandra made the best roast beef and Yorkshire pudding. This was a fun time of my life.

Backyard pool

My parents decided to put a pool in our backyard to give me some fun, physical activity after coming home from the hospital, or at least that was what I was told. I kind of remember there being a family vote about a pool or getting a cottage. I was the only one who voted cottage, as the other siblings were older and wanted to hang with friends, not family. I felt burned. Now, we wouldn't spend our summers camping as much, or that's what I thought.

We were putting a big deck around the pool, so Uncle Joe was using the table saw and cut his hand really badly. Apparently, he cut himself stopping me because my hand was close to being cut by the table saw.

I was really confused because my Uncle Joe was hurt, and my grandfather was mad and pounding the table. Memories like this create a lot of confusion for me. One must remember there was lots of drinking going on.

Shortly after this incident with Uncle Joe, my grandfather (dad's dad) died. I don't remember much about this death.

Grandmother, dad, and more stitches

I went with my dad to help my grandmother with yard work, and all she did was complain that I broke stuff both times I went to help her. I later refused to go see her.

We had BBQs all the time in the summer, and family would always come. It was fun.

It seemed like all of a sudden, mom started complaining more about how much dad was smoking and drinking. I remember thinking *if she would just not say anything, there would be no fights.*

I was out with a friend one day, and we swapped bikes. I really liked his bike—it was super fast. My friend had this rat trap for books on the back of his bike. We stopped, and I got too close to a wire sticking out of the rat trap, so it got hooked into my knee. If I recall, my friend ran home to get dad, and dad came and managed to get it out, but of course, I had to go get more stitches.

I remember when my dad was running across the field to get to me and pull my leg off the wire. I remember that this act of running actually gave me a sense of feeling cared for and loved, which was a rare occurrence, that's for sure.

Fun in the pool

We liked to have inner tube fights in the pool where we would stand on the tube and rock it till the other person fell off. Also, the pool was round, and we would walk around faster and faster, making it like a whirlpool to the point that no one could even stand up. These were a few fun memories I have of my childhood.

Glimpses of Calm in the Shit Storm

A camping trip was planned, but Gary, Lorie, and Doug were old enough to stay home, and they didn't want to go, so my parents, Ted and I went to a spot just outside of Toronto.

I was toasting a marshmallow, and when it caught on fire, I quickly blew on it. It slid off the stick and splattered all over my face. The burn on my face was taken care of, but when I went to bed in the tent, I saw sparks fly from the fire. I thought the tent was going to burn down. This was scary, and I never really felt like my parents cared for me.

Dad

I remember going fishing once with my dad up to Trenton. I felt special because it was just him and I. It was fun. I learned a little about the Trent Canal and got some much-needed time with just my dad. He was handy with stuff and taught me how to use power tools at a young age.

We made this little toy boat together. It felt good doing what felt like 'normal' stuff with my dad.

My dad did have a great garden full of strawberries, raspberries, and a lot of different kinds of veggies.

Dad was always busy working on something. He built a bathroom/laundry room downstairs in our house.

Dad's yard always had to be perfect. He was always cutting grass and pulling weeds.

And there was always drinking. Mom and dad would argue a lot about his drinking and smoking cigarettes.

My dad was pretty violent at times. I always thought if we just left him alone, he would be fine.

Mom

My mom had this big, blue car that she would drive to see her family in Stansted, Québec. We would go there and camp on this cool lake on the border of Vermont. We'd swim and have a lot of fun.

We brought home this huge dining room table from mom's aunt's house in Québec, and they had it refinished. It was a family heirloom.

The good guy

Lorie, my sister, dated this guy named Bruce. He was around all the time. He was Lorie's first boyfriend (from what I remember). He was fun, and everybody liked him.

When they broke up, I was confused. They seemed happy, and Bruce was liked by my family, so I wondered why he didn't stay with Lorie. I was young, but I was probably hoping this good guy would have stayed.

The bloody nose

When I was nine, my older brother Gary used his boss's van to take a bunch of us to the drive-in to see the movie *Jaws*. It was great.

I remember sitting on Gary's lap, and there was this intense part of the movie when the scientist (played by Richard Dreyfuss) went diving under a sunken boat in the middle of the night and pulled a shark's tooth out of the boat. Then, the head of the dead fisherman floated right out in front of him. I jumped back and gave Gary a bloody nose. Gary was focused on stopping his nose from bleeding, so he didn't get upset with me.

From that movie, I was even scared to swim in my pool, let alone open water. I didn't let anyone else know I was scared because that meant I would not be allowed to watch any other scary movies, and I would be teased like crazy.

Thanks, dad

I think I started Cub Scouts around this time, following in my brother Ted's footsteps. It was fun learning knots and going out in nature.

The only thing about all the fun stuff in Cub Scouts was that I was accident-prone, and if I was active, I was more than likely going to need stitches.

I went to Cub Scouts for about a year or two, but I was eventually kicked out. I couldn't go back unless my dad was involved. Well, that didn't happen, so I never went back.

Just not a loving family

Like I said, I was very accident-prone. I remember cutting my chin open on the mailbox hook and on the step railing. I'm not sure which one was first, but I had stitches both times.

I remember when I did this, I went into the dining room and said, "I think I need a bandaid," as I was bleeding badly. At that exact time,

My Perfect Storm

Lorie was about to go to her swim meet, so my mom made me go to the swim meet first, then to the hospital. The reminder that I wasn't really that important was something I felt often.

I remember feeling like I wanted to get even with my older siblings. They always bullied me and picked on me. So, I got this great idea that I did often. I deliberately opened a cupboard door so they would hit their head or walk into the door and then claim I didn't see them.

I remember being in Gary's car with him and his friend Scott. We drove by some other car, and I heard that Gary had ripped somebody off, so he had to duck down to not be seen. It was my job to sit by the window so Gary wouldn't be seen.

It was the summer of 1975, and Gary started talking about going to Calgary to work. Calgary seemed so far away. Aunt Cathy was also moving to California so she could attend school.

We had a big barbeque before they both left, and I only remember thinking I didn't want them to go. I was feeling a bit lonely and scared as I often felt like it was only Gary who protected me. He gave me some solace in living with this f'd up family of mine.

Aunt Cathy also gave me some reprieve. She would take me on small trips, and we would have fun. She would take me downhill skiing or just come pick me up for the weekend. I just knew I was safe, loved, and cared for when I was with her. I would miss her.

At this point in my life, I wasn't used to change and didn't like it. Why did Gary and Cathy have to move away?

CHAPTER 3

Intense, Turbulent Fronts

Everyone is leaving

Gary had been in Calgary for a few months before he returned home for Christmas. He got into a big fistfight with dad. They were both drunk, and dad had to get stitches in his forehead after Gary punched him.

I remember feeling scared because Gary was revving his car, and sparks were flying underneath. I was terrified. I thought it was going to blow up.

My feelings were so mixed up. I loved Gary because he showed me glimpses of love, but at the same time, this incident of fighting with dad terrified me. I was so lost.

In bed that night after Gary and dad's fight, I remember feeling lonely, lost, and scared about all the fighting that happened around me.

Frank

My Aunt Donna was dating this guy, Frank. They were into religious stuff, but they were a lot of fun. I felt safe when I was around them. I did lots of fun stuff with them. When we hung out with their church people, I didn't really fit in, though I did have fun. When they got married, I was their ring bearer. I was happy to do that. I liked Frank.

I remember when I was young, I went to a cottage Frank's parents owned. We went out on Lake Erie during the night in this big rubber dinghy boat. It was a blast, but I knew that if my parents knew I was out at night on these rough waters, they would have been really upset. There were a lot of us in the boat, and the bottom blew out, so we all flew everywhere. It was scary and fun at the same time.

My other aunt, Janet, was dating this guy named Dave Kraft. I thought this was funny because it always reminded me of Kraft food. They got married, and I liked them a lot too.

Violence was king

The biggest thing I remember about growing up was all the violence in our house.

Intense, Turbulent Fronts

It felt like Ted tortured me all the time. He called me stupid and bullied me. When it was just the two of us at home, I was scared. However, I learned to be mouthy back and bug him till he had to beat me. I know—fucked up, eh?

I don't remember there ever being consequences for Ted beating me up. What I saw was mom getting in between Ted and dad and protecting Ted from my dad. But when Ted beat me, he never got punished. It was all so confusing.

Seeing mom not have consequences for Ted, knowing how he hurt me, told me my mom didn't love me. And that's what I learned over and over again.

Life was lonely.

Ted

Violence was normal in my house. Ted and Doug would fight all the time. I remember one time, we were in mom's car, and they got into a fistfight. I just remember being scared sitting there in the front seat as they fought in the back seat. I clearly remember we were parked at the Zeller's parking lot, and mom must have been in the store. I was scared that I would be dragged into it. It was not a loving place to be.

There was no safety at home. I never knew when Ted and I would get into an altercation. I never felt safe. My mom often told me, "You were such a nice kid before the accident. Now look at you; you're just a little puke." I got this over and over again.

There were times when Ted would torture me and dump pepper in my nose, then put me in the dryer or the freezer.

My Perfect Storm

I remember stealing 10 dollars from him to buy a bunch of junk food for lunch at school. The school called home to ask where I got the money. I got a good spanking for this.

Friends

I learned early on that I couldn't even trust friends. Tim, one of my friends, blackmailed me for money. He was going to tell my parents what I had done. I don't remember what I had done; I was just scared my dad would find out, but I thought I was supposed to be able to trust my friends. I guess not. I can remember some details, like where it took place.

I remember the big swing set and monkey bars at the park where the school was. I also had lots of fun in a big forest near the school where my friends and I would play.

There was a catholic school beside my public school. I didn't know what that meant at the time. I mean, why did kids need to go to different schools? We're all just kids.

As the fifth kid in the family, all my clothes were hand-me-downs. The worst was the blue bell bottom cords; I would trip on the legs and fall because the bottoms were so big. I remember the kids at school teased me about them.

Resist

Grade four was when I started getting into lots of trouble. I was sent to the office all the time for fighting and teasing other kids. I remember my punishment was to sit with the kids I was bullying. Kind of messed up.

Intense, Turbulent Fronts

I remember getting the strap several times at school. It was always on the palms of my hands. It hurt like hell, but I never showed that it hurt.

Fucked up

My mom's pet name for me, Little Puke, was coming out more and more. She liked to say, "You're nothing but a little puke."

She proudly reminded me that I was supposed to be a girl and seemed to drill that into me so I would never forget it. I was now starting to understand my place in this world. I was a dumb kid and had become damaged beyond repair. Almost everyone let me know this. This was my life now.

Misunderstood

Most times my family had get-togethers, there were always fights, arguments, and drinking. All this became a normal way of life for me and my family. It also became normal for me to see that men should drink. I knew when I grew up, I would drink, fight, and take no shit from anyone.

I was now realising I was being left out of a lot of things, as I was the youngest of my cousins. I was getting bored when going to my aunts and uncles.

So, what happens when a kid is bored? They get into trouble, and that was me.

I would get shipped up to Kitchener all the time to hang out with my grandfather, mom's dad. I did like spending time with my grandfather, and I have lots of fond memories of him. I remember one Christmas, he spoiled us. He bought me a train set.

The arcade

It was around the time when arcades were becoming popular. There was an arcade at the local bowling alley near my house.

At the arcade, I discovered the games *The Galaxy* and *Pac-Man*. I had a lot of fun playing these games; however, it was at this time that I really started noticing I was different. I wasn't like the other kids. I didn't fit in.

One of the rich kids who came to the arcade would always be at the games I wanted to play. He had lots of money, so he hogged the machines a lot and bragged about all the stuff he had at home.

Watching that 'rich' kid play as much as he wanted while I was standing there in my hand-me-down clothes made me feel like a real outsider, and no one ever saw how much this was destroying me.

I was at a point in my life where I was old enough to venture out by myself and be out longer. At the arcade, this rich kid was wearing those expensive Kodiak boots, the kind only rich kids could afford. I remember smoking and being pissed off because he was hogging a game, so I dropped my smoke into his boot. It burnt him so he stopped playing and then I could play.

I was starting to see that the only way I was going to be seen or heard was to be the 'bad kid.' Well, that was what I was told I was. At least that way, I would get things to go my way.

Intense, Turbulent Fronts

More stitches

One day, my mom and I went shopping and when we came home, I cut my foot on the corner of the screen door, rushing to go to the bathroom. Doug was in the bathroom and wouldn't let me in, so I was bleeding all over the carpet. Off to the hospital for more stitches.

CHAPTER 4

Growing Intensity

Terrorizing with the twins

I was hanging out with my friends, Tim and Tom (twin brothers), a lot. They would fight all the time, but if you messed with them, you were in trouble. I see now that I liked hanging out with them because they were consistent in my life, or at least their reactions were consistent, so I knew what to expect.

I was at their house one day, whittling some wood, when I cut my knuckle with the knife. Yes, off to the hospital for more stitches.

We hung out all the time with my other friend, Lenny. They didn't like this other guy, Jerry, so I had to hang out with him separately.

One thing that stuck out for me about Jerry was he would get stressed and bite his hand all the time. It was strange. He got a scar on his hand from biting it so much, which we teased him about. And yes, bullying just became the norm for me. That's what was expected from me.

We were bullies. We terrorized the girls, kids smaller than us, and anyone else we could.

There was this girl named Samar. My buddies and I terrorized her all the time. Teachers would punish us for doing this by splitting us up and making some of us sit by Samar.

I remember another girl with special needs. We terrorized her a lot, too. We chased her and teased her. That was the norm for me.

I quickly came to learn that we would do anything to get a rise out of other people at school. I spent a lot of time in the hallway and the principal's office.

Before 10

I remember going camping up at Kill Bear Park. My big left toe, which had no muscle from the accident, just hung down. I would stub it all the time, and I remember stubbing it badly on some rocks.

This incident stands out for me because it felt like I was being held back again.

Back at home, Ted and I fought all the time, and he would beat me a lot.

Since the accident, I found my mom watching me like a hawk. Always ready to catch me in the act of doing something bad, like hurting myself again. There were a lot of things I wasn't allowed to do, like hockey, for fear of injuring myself again.

The slingshot

I remember having a cool slingshot, and Jen, this Asian girl from school, was teasing me that I couldn't hit anything. She stuck her ass out when she was on the top of the slide, and I nailed her in the ass. I loved that slingshot, and it was fun to use.

My train

Dad was one person in my life that did give me some good memories of my past. We built this cool train set from the original set my grandfather gave me. Our design had mountains, houses and a train station.

Dad made it so the table could be flipped up into the wall. That was a great memory of dad and the time he took to show me love. I also really liked that every Christmas, my grandfather would give me more stuff for my train set.

Always in trouble

I was always getting in trouble with the foul language that came out of my mouth. I remember we were hanging out down by a local variety store (Ted's Variety), and some man started to yell at us. I yelled, "Fuck off." He chased me and spanked me real hard.

A week later, the cops showed up. I thought I was in trouble for sure. They questioned me about what happened, and they wanted to charge the man who spanked me. My dad said no to this. I thought I was going to get a whooping again, but I didn't. My dad told me never to swear and have respect for people.

All this chaos really confused me.

I woke up one night hearing Ted screaming in pain and dad screaming at Ted. I heard the whip of the belt, and Ted started screaming more. I was scared that I was next, but dad never came in. I found out later Ted got caught stealing some stuff.

Ted and I were not the only ones who fought. Doug and I got into many scraps, too. One time, I had gotten into a fight with Doug over some disagreement. Within a short time, he discovered his pet fish went missing, and of course, he assumed I did something with it, so he beat me up. Sometime later, I found the fish lying on the floor dead. I hadn't done anything to his fish. It wasn't me.

Not fair

When Doug left, he left my parents with the remainder of the bill for the van that they had previously helped him buy. So, whenever I wanted to buy something, there was always the excuse of, "Well, we need to pay off Doug's car bill, so no, we can't get you what you want, Scott."

Ted and I were now the only kids left at home.

Growing Intensity

When Ted and I were at home, he would beat me up all the time, and he never had consequences. My mom would protect Ted from getting in trouble with my dad, which wasn't fair.

I felt like no one cared. All the people who cared had moved away or lived far away. At one point, I decided to run away and go to Calgary. All I thought was at least Gary would be there to protect me and take care of me.

At the age of 11, I convinced a travel agency to sell me a plane ticket for when school ended. I said my parents were in Calgary, and I was staying with a friend till school was over. However, one of my friends told Ted, and Ted went to the travel agency to tell them what I was doing, so that plan got kiboshed.

Out of my control

My dad had made the decision to stop drinking. He was not a happy man. He would sigh under his breath all the time, and when my friends heard him do that, they would tease me about it. I felt like even though things like that were out of my control, I was still punished for it. And I felt ashamed of my family.

I was woken up from my sleep, startled by my uncle's loud voice. Uncle Joe came over and started a fight with my dad. He was yelling that he wanted one of my dad's guns. He wanted to go shoot someone at work. Chaos and uncertainty were now my life. I guess that's the way life was to be. And I was learning that violence solved everything.

Holding hands

I was riding my bike home one day and rounded a corner. mom and dad were walking hand in hand. I still remember being shocked because I never saw signs of love and intimacy from them. This was really confusing for me because, for the most part, love wasn't a dominant feeling in my life.

BMX

After my family had dinner one night, I went out and saw that my BMX bike was stolen right from the backyard. I was heartbroken. I later found out who stole it, and when I told my dad and brothers about it, no one would help me get it back. Once again, I was reinforced that no one really loved me.

Can you believe at age 11, I surmised that my life sucked and wasn't fair? I wished I had been born into a different family. I was a loser. No one cared for me, and no one protected me. I felt so alone.

The beginning of addiction

Over the next few years, other than Ted beating me up, those years were ok.

I had to fight with my mom about stuff I wanted, and I would always get the cheapest of whatever it was. I got away from home as much as I could. I had to fight for everything I got.

Around age 11, my dad started taking me to work. It was fun.

I got to make money and get away from the house; it kind of made me feel like a man! Since mom wouldn't get me anything, I could now get my own stuff with my own money. I now had some purpose in my life.

Geographical cure

I still got in trouble at school all the time. I got the strap in grade five again, and I was still in Special Ed all the time. I decided to ask my parents to transfer me to Pineland, the school I would be going to for grade seven anyway. They agreed with me, and off I went for my sixth-grade year. Looking back at this, I consider this my first 'geographical cure.'

This is the year things changed a lot for me. I got a little more freedom from home.

Bruce, my next-door neighbour, was my grade six science teacher at Pineland School. So, when I arrived at his class, I automatically called him Bruce, and he replied, "Scotty, don't call me Bruce. My name here is Mr. Shapka."

Of course, my back was up immediately. I replied, "Bruce, can you call me by my name? It's Scott."

This went back and forth till he told me to go to the office. The decision was made that I would go to Special Ed once again and not attend his science class. When the school made this decision, I again felt like I was being punished. It didn't make any sense to me. Why was he not expected to call me my proper name when I was demanded to call him Mr. Shapka?

The bully

Being the bully made it hard for me to fit in. There was a time when the biggest guy in my class and myself got into a fight, and I ended up fighting the whole class. They were helping their friend fight me, and again, I was the singled-out enemy.

My friends and I would ride our bikes to Bronte Creek all the time to go swimming, have campfires and cook hot dogs.

I was walking home from my friend Lenny's house one day, and the guy across the street came out and beat me up. Lenny's brother, Art, saw the guy beating me up and came out and stopped it. He made that guy stand there and get a beating from me without fighting back. All I remember thinking is, *Wow, somebody stood up for me. Someone supported me. I never get this at home.* If it was Ted, he would have helped the guy beat me up or cheered him on.

Some buddies

I met this guy, Jeff Morton, who was older than me. He was different looking, a little scary, but a nice guy. Jeff was born with some birth defects. Back then, they called it mongoloid.

One day, Jeff and I went to Zellers and got caught stealing Pink Floyd's album, *The Wall*. My dad was called. He came and got me and took me home. He took the belt to me and whipped me so badly that I remember my mom jumping down the stairs to drop-kick him away from me.

I got into fights all the time. I was bigger than most kids my age, so any time I was in a fight, I usually didn't lose.

Growing Intensity

I would tease and torment kids in class. The one game I would play was to tease this guy named Rob. He was allergic to bees, and under my breath, I would say, "Bee." I would do this till he lost his temper, flipped his desk, and got sent to the office.

I said what I wanted to say to whoever or whomever and whenever. At this point, I felt like it didn't matter what I did. I got in shit for whatever I did or said, and I was told "no" for just being me.

At school, I got caught chewing gum as I was walking out the door and was told to write lines. The time came when I was supposed to hand in my lines, and, of course, I didn't do them. The teacher gave me a choice to do them or go to the office. I got up and walked to the office. I refused to write them.

CHAPTER 5

Misleading Glimpses of Escape in a Destructive Storm

New friend Jerry

Since I was at a different school, I started hanging out with a new friend, Jerry. We would have sleepovers at each other's houses. For me, I needed to stay away from my own house because I felt unloved and unsafe there anyway.

Well, I came to learn it wasn't safe at Jerry's house either. Jerry's dad started molesting me, and it felt good even though I thought it was wrong. I was confused because someone was showing some sense of care and positive attention to me, but I knew it was all wrong, kind of like everything in my life.

I thought of telling my family, but I knew they would just ask me what I did, and I would be in trouble, or they would think it was my fault. I had nowhere to turn.

Since it felt good, I went back for more. I felt bad. I knew I was doing something I shouldn't be doing. One day, I just stopped being friends with Jerry and stopped going over to his house, so the abuse stopped with Jerry's dad.

My first joint

Close to the end of grade six, I smoked my first joint. This was what I had been looking for. It was like—BAM—all my problems were gone.

I felt better than I had in years. I felt whole and powerful, and I wanted more. Joints cost money, though. So, I had to steal to get more. I tried to cash one of my parent's checks in my bank account, but I got caught. I told some lies to get out of that, and they believed me. I was just told not to do it again. Well, that was easy.

Around this time, I was stealing money out of dad's wallet when he was in the shower. I would sneak in and just take it.

I also learned I could play mom and dad against each other and get them fighting. You see, on Fridays, I would ask my mom for my allowance, then go downstairs and ask my dad. I could drag them into an argument easily and then escape out the back door when things were heating up between the two of them.

On the second last day of grade six, a friend, Steve Daily, and I were down at the little creek by the school, having fun trying to get each other wet. He fell and cut the palm of his hand really badly, needing major surgery. Running up the hill towards school, he was saying to the teachers it was an accident. Because of what everybody came to think of me, I was blamed, sent home, and told not to return.

I felt robbed that day. It was an accident, and my friend Steve even said so. Because no one believed us, I missed out on the best day of school—the last day of fun and games.

After the incident, I went home and went straight to bed, terrified I was going to get a beating. This time, I knew for sure I was. When my dad came to my room, he talked to me and asked what happened. I said it was an accident.

He left, and I never got hit. I never got yelled at. I stayed in bed. I was so confused and still terrified that he would come back because that's what always happened to me.

My dad came back to my room a little while later and asked me, "Why are you staying in your room?" I don't remember my reply, but I soon felt it was safe to go out.

My sister's wedding

My sister Lorie decided to return to Ontario from Calgary to have her wedding. Gary also came back to attend the wedding.

My Perfect Storm

The wedding was a great time. It was the first time I drank. I don't remember much of the night except I had rye and coke. Mom would catch me with a drink and take it off me, but my uncle would just give me another one. I loved being drunk because I felt like I had no problems. No cares. I wanted more of this.

Over the summer, my parents had lots of meetings about me with the school. After the incident at the end of grade six, they sent me to a shrink, and I acted out when I was there too.

Getting sued

My friend's parents, the friend who had the accident on the second last day of school, got themselves a lawyer. They were suing my parents, the Halton School Board, and the city of Burlington. My life was a mess.

My mom used this lawsuit to punish me. I didn't get things I wanted, and I wasn't allowed to do anything, either. My mom loved putting me down, and all of this was just killing me inside. I was getting high every chance I could.

My friend Tim was living with his mom across town, so I would take the bus to see him. I liked hanging out with Tim.

The summer after grade six went by fast as I worked with my dad most of the summer.

I believe it was the summer of 1981. I was 13 when we had a family reunion in Burlington. I have some great memories from that reunion. My mom's aunt, Mary, brought her foster daughter, and we hit it off. We had sex. It was my first time. It felt good that someone cared about me. I spent lots of time thinking about her after they left.

Back to school

Summer was over, and I was back to school. The school assigned me to be in Special Ed, which meant I wasn't able to take the class I really wanted to be in—shop class.

I had been taken for testing with shrinks and other things the school wanted done.

At some point, I got tired of being treated differently than the other kids and stood up and walked towards the door. Miss Fraser stood up to block the door.

She asked, "Where are you going?"

My reply caught her off guard. I said, "I'm going home until you let me go to the same classes as everyone else."

She didn't let me leave. I was being punished for an accident that wasn't my fault.

I said to Miss Fraser, "We can do this the easy way or the hard way; however, I'm going home."

I exclaimed, "I want to be in shop class, and that's the only reason I want to be in school, so when you decide to let me in shop class with all the other kids, I'll come back. So, move, I'm going home."

Once again, not one teacher would stand behind me and support me in what I was asking for.

I went home after Miss Fraser moved out of the way, and my dad called shortly after I got home. He asked what I was doing, so I told him I wasn't going back till they let me into shop class.

Dad immediately said, "Go get your work boots out," and I was off working at the shop with dad the next day.

Even with all the chaos in my life, I still had the mindset that I had to work hard. I understood that I had to do a man's job, drink lots, and take no shit from anyone.

Going to work

Life was great at work. I did what was asked and was left alone, for the most part. Some of the guys there were tough. I was with the men, not like the crap from school.

Now, I was a working man who made some money to be able to buy cigarettes. It was easy back then to buy smokes at my age. Dad would give me a note to go out and buy them. I would just keep the note and later get more smokes for me. My dad knew I smoked, and that seemed to be ok with him.

My weed intake went up a lot. I wanted to be high all the time. During this time, Ted got a girl pregnant, and then they broke up.

Misleading Glimpses of Escape in a Destructive Storm

The shit disturber school

The school decided to send me to another school. My last few years of transition were crazy. In the same year, I went from grade six to Special Ed to a grade nine class of 12 kids in a shit disturber school.

To get to this new school, I had to take the bus all the way across town. More work for me to do for a shit life.

Our shit-disturber class went camping at Algonquin Park. I hated it because the teacher who took us was a probation officer, and he was a bully. We were out on the canoes, and he was getting me wet, splashing me with the paddle. When I tried to dump his canoe, he hit my hands with a paddle and just blamed me when I got mad. I left and refused to do anything else with them. Once again, the person with the power had all the control, even though they were wrong.

Tim

Tim and I were hanging out one day, throwing rocks at each other. He threw a rock, and I saw it coming, but I didn't react quickly enough, so it hit the end of the smoke I had in my mouth. It took my front tooth out.

My mom was so mad because I was her only kid that had perfect teeth. Also, she didn't believe me when I told her about how it happened. She thought I got into a fight.

So, I did the semester in that 'shit-disturber' school for half of my grade nine year, and then they moved me to General Brock High School for grade 10. General Brock was a trade school, and my mother worked in the cafeteria there. When I got there, my mother decided to leave that job.

I always found it odd that she quit. There were two other kids that had moms in the school. It made me feel like my mom didn't like me. Since I moved around so much, I was starting to feel like I didn't fit in anywhere.

With my mom always protecting Ted from my dad and never protecting me, I was scared at home and at school. I felt like she didn't love or care for me.

CHAPTER 6

Some Warmth

A new level of violence

Ted was dating Stacy Beaver. I started dating her younger sister, Tammy. The fighting between Ted and I hit a new level of violence. He would beat on me and then get too tired, so I would get up and yell at him or throw something at him, and then it would start all over again. This happened almost every other day.

We were watching TV, and something happened that made me snap, so I threw a bowl of popcorn at him. He held me by the shirt and wouldn't let me fall so he could repeatedly punch me in the face. When he did let me go, I fell to the floor, got up, called him a goof, and it all started again. This was the kind of shit we did a lot.

Stacy's dad got transferred to Calgary, so Ted went with them. I was so happy he was leaving, as we had been fighting for so long. I finally had the house to myself. It would be grand, but it made me sad that Stacy's sister was moving. Tammy was one person that showed me some sense of love.

I was lonely. Smoking weed was the main thing I did every day, and all the people I hung out with did the same thing. Smoking weed and getting into fights was all we did.

Sheri

At 13 years old, I was scared and lost, just starting grade 10. This cute little blond girl walked up and said, "You're Barbara Jo's Uncle, right?"

I replied, "Yes." She informed me she was Barbra Jo's Aunt, then asked if I wanted to go smoke a joint and of course, I said yes. Her name was Sheri.

Sheri always had weed. We smoked weed every day at school and went for lunch all the time. Everyone thought we were dating; however, we were not. I always had a soft spot for Sheri. She helped me escape from reality, and she was kind. She seemed to accept me for just me. I needed her at that time in my life.

At this point, I was getting loaded every chance I could. One morning, I came to school, and Sheri said, "Let's smoke a joint." She handed it to me. I lit it, and it went up because there was no actual weed in it;

it was just a bunch of matchheads, so it hurt my throat and lungs. I was mad and didn't talk to her for a while after that. However, these kinds of things seemed to happen a lot back then.

Just go to the Davis' house

I would go see little Barbra Jo all the time. I was allowed to drink at the Davis' house, so I would be there every weekend. I worked for my dad a lot, so I had some money. There was always drinking at the Davis' house, which was good for me. Drink and get away from home—a good combo. Anytime I had a fight at home, the Davis' house was a good place to go.

At 13, I stole my parent's car. On that day, my parents had gone to a wedding. I forgot it was a Sunday wedding, which meant they wouldn't be out drinking like crazy because they had to work the next day.

I had come back home with the car looking for more money, but they were there, so I got caught. All I did was tell them to fuck off, threw the keys at my mom, and left.

I went and stayed at the Davis' house for a week. I would drink any chance I got and smoke weed every day. I was out of control. I didn't want to feel. I smoked or drank to oblivion.

I remember going to school with a wineskin filled with rye. I got caught drinking in the hallway by a teacher. She turned her back for a second, so I left, went to my class, and hid there.

It was the last class of the day. I was leaving school, and my dad was there. He saw me and backhanded me in the face. I punched him back, told him to fuck off, and left for about 10 days. I went to the Davis' house to stay once again.

Suspended

I was suspended from school for 10 days. Nothing else was said about this. The stuff from my mom about me being a little puke continued. It was at this point I knew she didn't love or care about me. Fuck, no one did.

Tim and Tom had moved to Edmonton, but now they were back living with their dad in Hamilton, Ontario. I would bus it or hitchhike, whatever way I had to get there. I usually made it there faster by hitchhiking.

I would go to the horse track with Tim, Tom, and their older brother, John. He was old enough to be our parent. He was newly separated from his wife. I remember thinking back then—why would he waste all his money on gambling?

John would place bets for us. It was fun. The twins had been going for years, so they showed me how to bet. They were so excited when the race was on.

It was becoming my new normal to get stoned and drink with everyone in my life. I blacked out all the time. There were two guys I met at school who were older than me. They introduced me to acid. I loved it. The first week I tried it, I ended up doing it every day. I started doing more hits each day.

I was also smoking weed in welding class, using the air vents to not get caught.

Some Warmth

Dad's advice

My friend Lenny started ninth grade at the same time I started grade ten, but he had lots of other friends.

I bullied some of the guys that came into ninth grade. Grade niners were called Gummers; not sure where this came from. We made them push pennies with their nose down the hallway as a form of hazing.

In grade 10, there were these guys that bullied me a lot. One of them, Phil Henry, tormented me. I was scared of him. I made it through the year, hating the bullying, but realized school was definitely not my thing. I was learning you had to be tough and fight back.

I met this guy, Mark Barkly. We drank and smoked weed together. We stole a car stereo by breaking and entering. We got money and booze, so we went back to my house to divide up the cash and get drunk. The cops came looking for me, and my dad told them he would bring me down to the police station when I arrived home.

On the drive down, my dad said to me, "Now that you're getting in trouble with the law, maybe you should start watching how much dope you're smoking and go to class."

This was all that he ever said about the weed and getting in trouble with the police. My dad was cool. He left me alone.

Hanging with the boys

I was running my own life at 14. Nobody told me what to do.

Tim, Tom, their friend Mah, and I went to an Ozzy concert, and we decided to do acid on the way down to Detroit, Michigan, where the concert was being held. The twin's dad drove us there.

At the time, I was actually sitting right beside their dad, and I had to secretly take the little acid pill out of my pocket and sneak it into my mouth. We didn't want to take it across the U.S. border.

When we got over the border, I went to score some weed. When I was looking for the drugs, this big black dude stayed with me and helped me score because he said I would get hurt there and the cops would retaliate against the black people for a white Canadian kid getting hurt, so he looked out for me.

Back in T.O.

I went to Toronto to the horse track a lot with Tim, Tom, and Mah, and we would drink on the train going there. This one time, we lost all our money, so we had to hitchhike home. We were picked up on the freeway by the cops. All they did was take us to the bus station, which was closed.

The four of us slept in the park across the street from the bus station that night. It was scary. There was an alarm in a building that kept going off, and it was cold. In the end, we found out Tim had money on him. He finally told us, so we took the train home in the morning.

Some Warmth

Back in school

At school, the woodworking classroom was always cold, and there were no shop coats to wear, so I decided to wear my warm Mac coat (also known as the Canadian tuxedo). Mr. McGray was not happy with my choice to put on my own coat and told me to take it off. I refused. He sent me to the office, and on the way out, I called him an asshole.

As I was walking out the door, he punched the back of my head. I spun around and caught him with a hook to the chin, and down he went. I proceeded to the office, and when I got there, Miss Singleton, the Vice Principal, asked what I was there for. I told her, and I was suspended again.

They didn't let me back into woodworking class, so I was transferred to the electric shop.

By this time, I had the school, my parents, and siblings telling me I wouldn't amount to anything. I thought they were all right. I believed they were all right. I was always in a conflict, and I didn't have many friends.

Even the cops told my friends they should stay away from me. Ted and his girlfriend Stacy talked about how they thought I would spend my days in and out of prison. I even thought I would be dead before I was 25.

I was at school with no money, so I borrowed 20 bucks from a friend for some lunch. The next day, I was called to the office. When I got there, there were cops, and I got questioned about the $20 I had for lunch. I was lucky I had just finished the weed I had, or they would have found it when they searched me.

They were accusing me of stealing $20 from a teacher. I told them I wasn't even in her class yesterday. I skipped out. They didn't check; they just called my dad and told him they suspected me of stealing a wallet. I got home that night, and dad beat me badly. I was on his shit list for a while again after this day.

Eventually, the school figured out it was not me, but they never called to say that. I waited two or three weeks for them to call. They never did. I walked into Miss Singleton's office without asking, lost my shit on her, and told her how disrespectful they were for not calling my parents about that.

I felt like the rest of the world wanted me to show them respect, yet they didn't give me respect. This was just more ammo in my pocket to justify that no one cared.

I told Miss Singleton I quit school, grabbed a bunch of bus tickets from her desk, and left. There were six weeks until grade 10 was over. I still remember passing English, math, and other classes, but I failed gym.

The gym teacher put in the notes, "Scott is a well and capable student, but his six-week absence has caused him to fail." Not sure why he thought I was a capable student. I refused to run the track and do most of the activities in the gym class. The education system seemed messed up. They pass you on the hard stuff and fail you on the easy stuff.

Work is my life now

At that point in my life, I hardly went home, and when I did, it was when mom and dad weren't there or were asleep.

Some Warmth

One night, I came home around 4 am, which was a normal time for me. Dad was sitting in his Lazy Boy chair in the dark. He yelled at me and scared the shit out of me. He said if I wasn't going to school, I was going to work. Going back to work was fine by me. It gave me money to drink and smoke with.

A little bit of fun

Mom, dad, and I drove out west to see Doug and Lorie in Kindersley, Saskatchewan. I had a hard time being around my parents that much. I still couldn't smoke around my mom. Lorie was pregnant and had just split up with her husband, Jeff.

We continued to Calgary to see Ted and Stacy. We spent a few days there. At some point, I lost my shit with my parents and left. I got on Calgary Transit feeling lost and went to see Stacy's sister, Tammy Beaver. We had fun hanging out and catching up.

My parents drove up to see my brother Gary in Jasper, but I drove up with Ted and Stacy in their car. Gary lived in Prince George, and we all met in Jasper in the Rocky Mountains. It was pretty cool. We camped in Jasper for a few days. This was my first time in the mountains.

Gary and I had some time together, so we got stoned.

We all went to A&W to get something to eat. I was in the bathroom when dad came in and saw I was smoking.

He said, "Moms out there," and I replied, "I don't care anymore," and walked out with my smoke in hand.

When mom noticed I was smoking, she said, "You're smoking?" and I sarcastically replied, "Oh my god, I am?" and continued to smoke.

My parents and I left Calgary and headed back towards Burlington, picking up Lorie in Kindersley on the way. Since Lorie was pregnant, she decided to come back to Burlington so she could get help from our parents. It was nice to be able to ride in my sister's car to get away from my parents.

Bullshit again

When we got back to Burlington, I returned to work with my dad.

There was talk about me going back to school, but if I was to go back, I had to be good, no skipping, no trouble. I had to get a paper signed by every teacher for every class. I didn't like it. It was bullshit once again. I was being treated disrespectfully by the school system. Staying on the straight and narrow didn't last long.

Something happened to me that summer. I sprouted and got big. I had decided I wasn't taking any shit from anyone. Phil Henry and I got into a fight in auto body class, and I fought back. He shoved his fingers in my eyes, so I did the same, just harder. Mr. Powel broke the fight up fast.

Phil spent the next few days telling me I was dead on Friday. I was scared. He started shooting his mouth off at me in the cafeteria. Something snapped inside, and I lost my fear. I walked over to him, got in his face, smashed his food tray out of his hands and said, "You coward. Why wait till Friday?"

Some Warmth

We went out to the smoke pit and started fighting. His friends were trying to stand on my feet to help him. This was the last time he bothered me.

Things at home with my sister were bad. We argued all the time. I went to the Davis' all the time to see Barbra Jo and, of course, to drink and party so I didn't have to feel.

Lorie had her baby, Katie, and Lorie and I's relationship was really rough. One day, Katie was screaming in the car seat, sitting on the floor. I picked the car seat up to comfort Katie, and she stopped crying. Lorie came along and snatched the car seat, with Katie in it, out of my arms. I lost my shit and started yelling and swearing.

My dad stepped in and told me to stop swearing, but all I heard was him taking Lorie's side, so I kept it up. We got into a fight, and I fought back with everything I had. Dad hit me. I hit him back. Once again, I was doing something nice and ended up in a fight. I got blamed for everything, and they took each other's sides like normal.

Lorie moved out shortly after this. I had the house to myself again. It was great. Everything that went wrong was always pointed back to me like it was my fault. By this time, I was tired of my mom taking my dope, so if she took it, I either took her money to replace it or I took booze out of the mini bar in our house.

I no longer hid my drug use. There was nothing they could do anyway. Somewhere through the years, my dad taught me that if I lied, there would be consequences, and if I told the truth, there would be none.

I was the only child who didn't get beat by my dad as badly as the rest of them (or so I've been told). Ted beat me up more than my dad, and my mother was all about emotional abuse. I had heard that my mom told my dad if he beat me like the rest of the kids, she was going to leave him.

Something better?

Ted had moved home from Calgary, and we actually got along a little better. I had gotten bigger and was never around much. I was getting loaded all the time and drinking as much as I could get my hands on. I was able to go to the liquor store and the beer store at 15, so I was drinking whenever I wanted.

I found when I took LSD (acid), I could drink more, so I took LSD every week. I had learned that to be a man, you had to fight and drink, and then no one can fuck with you or else they pay the consequences.

During the summer when I was 15 years old, I planned a party when my parents were away. I brought home two cases of beer for four of us. With 48 beers, ready to party, Ted started to make a fuss about it. We came to an agreement, and we put 24 beers away.

I didn't really like that Ted was making rules for my party; however, I was willing to roll with it.

Lorie came over, and when she found out minors were going to be drinking in the house, she threatened to call the cops.

Already drunk, I lost it and went after her when she said, "I will call the cops." Ted stepped in and tackled me to the floor, and all I remember thinking about was all the beatings he had given me over the years. All I thought was, *this fucker isn't going to beat me ever again.*

Some Warmth

I saw the knife drawer and went for one. By this time, my friends were there helping Ted by trying to take the knife away from me. I got him in the arm and myself badly in the leg. Somehow, things broke up.

I went downstairs to get more beer. At this point, I was in and out of a blackout. I left the house and walked down to the ghetto to a friend's house who was much older than me. I was drunk out of my mind, and I asked him for a bandage.

The next thing I remember was that I was in his kitchen, and he was ripping up bed sheets. I was wondering why. He said I was bleeding out. I looked down, and there was a massive pool of blood on the floor. I just went back to drinking my beer. The cops showed up at my house, and they followed my trail of blood to my friend's house in the ghetto.

I was taken to the hospital, stitched and bandaged up, and then taken to the juvenile centre. I was so angry. They put me in a cell.

The next day, I went to court, and they transferred me to a minimum security centre. It was boring. I hated it, but I knew if I was an asshole there (and fought this system), there would be less hope for me, so I played the game of being 'good.' I didn't want to be there longer and just wanted to be out so I could drink and party. At this point, my leg was so sore I could barely walk.

CHAPTER 7

A Positive Glimpse Amongst the Damage

Court ordered

Before I even turned 16, I went to court a few times, and it was decided I wasn't allowed home. I was sent to a group home in Oakville, the town next to Burlington, where my parents were. I had to share a room with someone else. I was lonely and didn't fit in again.

My Perfect Storm

My uncle Arnie called and said he was sorry to have to tell me he found my dog, Lady, dead. Another thing that sucked. Lady was something good growing up.

I was court-ordered to go to either Alcoholics Anonymous (which is a program to help stop drinking) or adapt. So off to A.A. I went.

Things looking up

From General Brock School in Burlington to General Wolfe School in Oakville, I now knew no one.

I was so pissed off and angry because I was the one reaping the punishment, and Ted was the one who beat me all the time, yet he never got kicked out of the house. I beat him once, and I was kicked out.

I went to one A.A. meeting, and there was this pastor or a priest telling his story. All I could think about when the pastor spoke was, *I'm not going to church.*

I turned 16 years old. I was living in a group home. Life sucked. I was alone, stupid, and no one loved me.

Living at the group home was nicer than living at my own home, at least. I attended school regularly and attempted to stay on the straight and narrow.

I had gotten a job working at a grocery store and was working a lot. I was happy to be making money again. On my way home one night, walking in the rain, a car drove by and soaked me.

A Positive Glimpse Amongst the Damage

The next day in homeroom, I was sitting beside Marcelle, who was laughing about being in a car last night and soaking someone when they drove by. So, I told her it was me. They all laughed. It was funny. Kind of nice to laugh again.

I had to pay a little rent at the group home. School was going ok, and I started smoking weed again.

Writing lines

I met this guy, Graham. We would get stoned together all the time. We got into lots of trouble together, too. His mom was a teacher at a private school where all the rich kids went.

One day during homeroom, we were sitting with two girls at the back table. The girls and Graham were talking through the Lord's prayer, and we were all told to write lines of the prayer. A week went by, and we didn't get the lines done, so we were given a choice to do them or go to the office. Off to the office we went.

Well, of course, this happened on a morning when Graham and I were stoned on acid, and the other girls came to school stoned, too.

So, when we went to the office, the principal (a guy known as 'Chrome Dome') gave us a lecture.

He asked, "What do you have to say for yourselves?"

Of course, out of my mouth came, "I think she (the teacher) needs a fucking hearing aid cuz I wasn't talking, and I'm not writing the lines."

We all broke out laughing, so we were told to either write them or be suspended. So, we wrote one page, photocopied them in the library, and handed them in.

Fuck the rules

The friends I was just getting to know were all going to the drive-in movie theatre at the last minute. It was the first time I had been asked out since I started school. This was a bright light for me. I was starting to make friends.

Because I was still at the group home, I needed to ask to stay out late to go to the drive-in. One of the group home staff said, "You know the rules. You must put in your request on Wednesday if you want to go out late on Friday."

I was so pissed. Life is bullshit, so I decided to go anyway and pay the consequences.

Not even sure what movie we went to, but when I got home late, the door was locked, so I had to knock to get in. The dick employee opened the door and asked where I had been. He then asked if I was stoned, and I said, "Yes," as the 'fuck it' button was pressed.

He said, "Go to bed. We'll deal with this in the morning."

I woke up thinking *fuck this* and left. I hitch-hiked to Hamilton and stayed with my dad's sister for a night or two. My parents came and got me and took me home.

A Positive Glimpse Amongst the Damage

Back home

I stayed at home, and life just went back to the way it was. I got loaded as much as I could. At this point, I decided not to go back to school. Not much point.

The school decided to let me get credits by working at Neil's Auto Body. Things were going well. I asked my mom to help me buy a motorcycle. She said she would never help her kids buy a motorcycle. I ended up buying a cheap one that needed to be worked on all the time.

Tim, Tom, and Lenny had bikes as well; they even had dirt bikes as kids.

Within two weeks, mom, Ted and I were at the motorcycle shop. Ted was looking at buying a bike. Mom ended up co-signing a loan for him to get a bike. *Oh my fuckin' god*.

I was mad. She just told me a few weeks back that she would never help her kids buy a motorcycle, and now she was co-signing a loan for Ted to get one. This was just confirming that she really didn't love me.

I decided I wouldn't talk to her anymore. She would ask me something and I would say nothing, or I would tell her, "You lost the right to talk to me."

Mom went to my dad and asked him to talk to me. He told her she caused the problem, so she should fix it with me.

Bruce

At this point in my life, I did whatever I wanted.

Bruce next door would always call the cops on me when we were partying at the house or when we would race up and down the street on our bikes. I had the corner basement bedroom in our house, and it had two windows facing Bruce's house. I would go home, put my speakers in the window, crank the tunes, and wake up his young kids. I liked to piss him off.

He went to my dad and complained. However, my dad told Bruce he created the problem and that he wasn't getting involved.

Bruce continued to call the cops, and we had lots of arguments. I kept waking up his kids with my loud music.

Mom kind of did something nice

One day, my motorcycle broke, and my mom agreed to help me buy a better one. Although she later accused me of never giving her any payments, which was so fucked up. I promised myself that with this bike, I wasn't going to drink and ride.

The first night, I got so hammered, so the promise I made that day of no drinking and riding didn't last long. I was so drunk I had my friends help me get my bike off the sidestand, and I rode home.

I woke up the next morning and almost automatically looked to see if I had road rash and then looked to see if the bike was home. There were lots of mornings I couldn't recall how or when I got home.

A Positive Glimpse Amongst the Damage

At the age of 16, I was blacking out all the time. It was fun working at my dad's shop and riding around getting high with my friends.

A bunch of friends were at my place, and we did acid. There were no initial effects, so Lenny and I decided to go score something to smoke to help it fire and get the trip going.

On the ride to score, the acid kicked in. I was so stoned.

Steve, the guy we were buying from, wasn't home, so we left and ended up in an accident that was my fault. Steve showed up when we were picking our bikes up, so we scored weed off him.

Len's house was closer, so we went there to fix the bikes. Len hurt his knee badly but avoided going into his house because he didn't want to get caught being stoned. His mom saw me and dragged me into the house to clean the road rash that I had.

Len spent the rest of the summer riding with a cast on.

Proud, I guess

That summer, I was drinking all the time. I believe I got five fines for drinking (under age). Each for $53. I was proud of all of them.

I quit my job at Neil's Auto Shop because I had problems with the owner and went to work at my dad's shop. Getting back to work meant more money, which meant more drugs.

I would buy a fiver of oil (drugs for my buddies and I) and sell half and smoke half. This way, it was almost free. Selling drugs and having an increase in my wages, I was making good money.

My Perfect Storm

Priorities, right?

I wanted to buy parts for my motorcycle, but drugs and alcohol came first. So, it never happened.

That winter, I got my first car. It was a pile of junk but a car. I was a man now because I owned my own stuff.

Mr. Bluhm (Lenny's dad) helped me fix my crappy car to get it on the road. I wished my dad would help me with this stuff, but he didn't know much about car mechanics.

My friends and I partied a lot in that car and went tobogganing and drank our asses off. This one time, we were tobogganing in Lowville, and I was doing acid. I discovered that if I did acid, I could drink more.

So, one night, freezing rain came, and we had to push the car up the hill, leaving Lowville. On the way down the other side of the hill, I was driving, and we did 360s all the way down. I managed to keep the car on the road. Everyone was saying what a good driver I was. Stoned on acid and drinking, my eyes were shut the whole time. I threw a beer up, and it landed on Tammy's lap. Tammy was the girl I was dating.

I wasn't nice to Tammy. I'm not sure why she stayed with me. I embarrassed her into having sex with me and then got her pregnant the first time we were together. I was so drunk I only thought of what I wanted.

The day we were going to tell her parents, Tammy got busted at school selling my oil. Tammy was clingy, and I was scared, so I ran, drank, and popped more pills. I didn't even know what I was taking most of

A Positive Glimpse Amongst the Damage

the time. I'm not sure how Tammy told her parents she was pregnant and what their reaction even was.

I was angry and resentful. I pushed Tammy out of my life. I drove home from Hamilton one night so drunk I remember swerving from one side of the road to the other, throwing up on the passenger seat.

I was drunk all the time. I got my first impaired charge, so I was off the road for three months. I remember yelling at the cops, "It doesn't matter. I won't live past 25 years old anyways."

CHAPTER 8

What a Fool to Think I Could Escape the Storm

Just got to run away

I was scared about Tammy being pregnant. I had to get away. I went to my brother Doug's place in Saskatchewan.

Doug arranged a ride out to Saskatchewan for me. So here I was a drunk, running away from my problems.

I got a job working on the pipeline as a welder's helper. I drank every day to oblivion.

I was angry that I had nothing. I was dumb, as I've been told over and over again.

Bar brawl

Some of the new friends I had met while at Doug's went to a different town to a dance, and a big bar fight broke out. Doug ended up there, and I got beat up badly.

Doug pushed me in the trunk of his car to save me from being really hurt in the fight. I was mad at him. How dare he not let me fight.

When we got back to the house, I threw a suitcase through his window because I was so angry. I was so drunk that night that I think I actually slept in a ditch. We eventually worked things out.

Mmmm mushrooms

Doug had some friends come over. They had been to British Columbia to pick mushrooms. This was my first experience, and it was great.

I ate way too many mushrooms. We went to the town fair, and the band Chilliwack was playing. I drove home drunk in a blackout. I almost drove the truck into a slew, which meant I would have been stuck in a big pond and might have drowned.

What a Fool to Think I Could Escape the Storm

What I understood was that I was running from myself. I was a loser. I was drinking as much as I could to escape. If people would have left me alone, I would be fine.

Gary and Gloria

With things not working so well at Doug's in Kindersley, I headed to Prince George, British Columbia. Gary lived in Prince George with his wife, Gloria. Gary and Gloria had just had their first daughter, Mary.

I got a job at Convoy Supply as a dock hand. I had money to drink, and that meant I would fit in with what Gary did. We drank and partied all the time and just spent time together drunk. Gloria did not like me. I was unreliable and got Gary drinking more than she liked.

My dad called and told Gary and I that my mom left him. He said, "Don't come home. You'll just be in the way."

Randy James

A few weeks later, I got a call from Tammy saying my son was born. Tammy named him Randy James.

I was a drunk and didn't see myself as any help to Tammy, and she never required anything from me, so I continued on with what I was doing. Drinking, drugging, and just figuring out how to get more.

The bosses at work kept warning me about my drinking and my performance as a dock hand, and then they fired me.

My dad didn't want me back in our home as it always felt like mom and dad blamed me for their split up.

The trip home

I decided to go home anyway. I took a bus. What a trip (literally). I was smoking weed and being obnoxiously loud on the bus. This old guy gave me four pills and said, "Only take two of them." And what did I do? Took all four. I slept, and I slept, and I slept.

I was back living with dad in our family home as it was mom who left the house when they split up. Dad took me to work, so I had a job right away.

Dad and I would stop at the bar on the way home every night to have dinner and a few beers. From the bar to the beer store to home—that was my life.

Shortly after I arrived at dad's house, I contacted Tammy, and she let me see Randy a few times.

I had learned that she was actually a virgin the first time we had sex. It really sucks that her first time was with an asshole like me. With my drunkenness, she stopped letting me see Randy. I don't really blame her.

The ministry took me to court for child support, and I had to pay about $60 a month until he was legally adopted by the man who was raising him as his son. I was never any kind of a man. I ran from everything.

Things got so bad that I was getting blamed for my dad's drinking. My family often made me feel guilty for encouraging my dad to drink, as we often drank together.

What a Fool to Think I Could Escape the Storm

My house was the party house. I was even blacking out so badly that I thought I had missed a full day's work, but I was actually there and had no recollection of it.

The guys from work would go to the bar for lunch on Thursdays and Fridays, and I thought it was strange that they ordered food. Why would you want food that just filled your belly? Less room for beer. I would have six beers and go back to work, smoking weed all day long.

This bender had to come to a halt at some point.

Suicide

I progressively did more and more acid. Me and my buddies were at the house partying and playing drinking games with tequila. I decided I wanted to do more acid than I had ever done before, so I snorted a big line of it after I had already consumed lots of it.

I continued to drink, went to work, and came home on a Friday night to a party at the house. I managed to pass out for an hour or so. We had enough beer to last till the store opened at 11 am. I drove my dad's car up the road, and I couldn't feel the seat or the steering wheel. The yellow line was moving even though I was on a straight road.

I got to the beer store, and there were cops there. I just drove up, went in, and bought cases of beer. That night, I was so spun out from the drugs and booze, hating life, that I started to take my dad's sleeping pills. I didn't come down, so I took more till I consumed the whole bottle. This was a real low for me, and looking back, I guess it was my first attempt at suicide.

One of my buddies, Dave, saw the empty bottle of sleeping pills in the bathroom. He confronted me about it. I was telling everyone to leave so I could go to sleep. Somebody called the cops, and an ambulance was called, too. The cops came, and I ended up in the hospital, getting my stomach pumped.

I was mad. I was fucking having the perfect high. If people would just leave me alone, I would be fine. I got transferred to detox.

Yellow

Three days later, Ted's wife, Dee, brought me some clothes and told me I looked like crap. I looked in the mirror for the first time and saw I was yellow.

Alcoholics Anonymous came in and put a meeting on. Uncle Joe came and saw me and took me to my first outside meeting, as he was sober and going to meetings.

I knew something wasn't right about how I drank or the things I did. The A.A. people were nice to me. Even the people in detox were nice to me. It had been a long time since I experienced this.

My first sponsor

I met Brian, who later became my first sponsor. He would say things like, "If you drink again, you'll go to jail, lose your licence, beat your wife, or worse." I thought, *not me*.

After about a week in detox, I was let out. My life was starting to shift. I was going to meetings every day. I was back to work, and I rented my first apartment.

What a Fool to Think I Could Escape the Storm

Sober sex

A girl from one of the A.A. meetings showed up at my house late one night. It was great sex, and I was sober. It was amazing. We were up all night. I had to work the next day with no sleep.

I was scared and lonely all the time and didn't know what I was doing. I had no help from my family. I was attempting to trust people at the A.A. meetings.

When I attended the meetings, it was thought that newcomers had nothing to share and they were just supposed to listen and talk to their sponsor.

I had no wheels at this point, so I went to my mom's house and asked to borrow her car to go to a dry dance in Toronto on a date with the girl from the A.A. meeting. We were out late before I dropped her off at home.

I took the car back to mom's house. I decided to just let myself in, but she woke up and said I couldn't stay there. I saw from the door she had a man in bed with her.

How could she not let me stay there? It proved to me, once again, that she didn't love me. I had to walk an hour back home to my apartment.

I was a basket case. I was having a hard time coping without drugs and alcohol. I was depressed, unloved, and feeling lonely.

I was now the big fuckup even though I wasn't drinking. I quit working for my dad and went to work for Len's brother, Art, at a gas station he owned.

My Perfect Storm

Things were going pretty well for me until I went to a party with Art and smoked a joint. Within a week, I was back drinking and out of control.

My life was over

I moved in with this guy I met when I was working with him (when I was with a temp agency) for a short while, and he was trying to keep his townhouse as he was separated from his wife. I rented the basement room from him to help him keep his townhouse. I tried getting work and was drinking when I could.

I was a loser.

I tried getting a painting job and didn't get it.

I was riding a bike with no insurance on it.

Desperate for booze, I robbed a 7-11. I got caught. My first trip to jail.

They put me in the range for first-time offenders. These guys were loud and out of control. I fought all the time and would beat them up until they moved me out of the area I was in.

They moved me up to the pen range, where there were inmates who were serving longer sentences. It was quieter and more what I liked. The guards thought that putting me in the pen range meant I could be taught a lesson and would get some of my own medicine. However, I knew how to fit in.

What a Fool to Think I Could Escape the Storm

Nobody would help me get bail. My mom said, "Look at yourself". I was in the pre-sentence for months at the Barton Street Remand Centre and then was sentenced to two years less a day plus probation after the time was served.

I was sent up to Guelph Reformatory to do my two years. My life was over.

I was transported in a van with about six others. It was scary driving to the reformatory for the first time, not knowing what to expect. It was a big, old, stone building. I had read a book called *Go-Boy!* by Roger Caron on this reformatory, and it was not a nice place.

Inside, I found weed like I was on the street. I went to a few A.A. meetings to make myself look good and get parole. Got into a few fights and ended up in the hole once for 10 days for fighting.

After eight months, I was granted parole with stipulations like no drinking or drugs and to do a 28-day treatment. I got high the day I got out of the treatment centre.

Québec

My family decided to help, so I was going to stay with my aunt Mary in Québec. The plan was that I was going to work for my mom's uncle in his granite quarry.

Off I went once again to live a new life somewhere else I didn't know anyone.

It was lonely but also a little exciting living in the small town of Stanstead, where everyone knew everybodies business.

My Perfect Storm

Working with my uncle didn't pan out, so I got whatever work I could. I didn't drink, but everyone I was hanging out with was doing coke, so I started doing it, too. Thankfully, that didn't last long.

Doing coke led me back to the drink. I hid this for a while, and then Ted offered me a job framing houses. I talked to my parole officer, and he made arrangements for me to go back to Hamilton so I could work with Ted.

I missed the guys I grew up with and had lost touch with most of them. I was lonely and drank alone a lot. No one knew I was drinking yet again.

Back in Hamilton, my family was having Christmas dinner at my mom's. I showed up so drunk I went straight to bed. The cops had followed me home as I had been driving. They questioned my family but never questioned me. That's all that happened.

I was out of control again, but I knew I needed to work so I could keep drinking.

The people I hung out with were getting rougher and rougher.

I was over at the Davis' getting drunk with Dave. He passed out, and his girlfriend Sheri started kissing me. I had wanted this for a long time.

Sheri and I had sex that night. I woke up in the morning, not even sure what exactly happened with Sheri and I. I was racked with guilt for what I did to Dave by sleeping with his girl.

Within about six months, Sheri left Dave and Sheri and I started dating. I called my parole officer and said I was staying in Hamilton. He said I had to come back to Stanstead to finish some paperwork.

What a Fool to Think I Could Escape the Storm

I told him, "If I come back, I will lose my job."

I decided to stay in Hamilton, so an arrest warrant was put out for me. I got popped going the wrong way down a one-way street. I was arrested and taken back to Barton Street Jail.

From my cell, I could see the apartment Sheri and I lived in. They put me back up on the pen range. There was talk that everyone knew I would be getting out soon, and they wouldn't keep me in here for long, but if you had a short sentence, you were not welcome on the pen range.

I was asked to leave, and I said to the guy who asked me, "Thanks."

He replied, "Huh?".

I replied, "If I asked you to leave, I would knock you out first and drag you up to the grill.

He came back to me and said, "Scotty, you can stay. We like you."

He then went and knocked some other guy out and dragged him to the grill where the guards would see him.

Within two weeks, I got out and returned to work with Ted.

I was great at framing houses. I drank almost every night and on the way to work in the morning.

I was back with Sheri, and we fought all the time. My drinking was a problem.

I stopped drinking

We lived on the 19th floor, and because of our fighting, I decided to move out. She decided to throw my suitcase over the balcony. I stopped drinking.

I ended up moving back in after a week or so. After a few weeks, she had bought me a case of beer because I was a sober asshole. So off I went again. I was drinking all the time, even in the morning before work and on the way to work.

Things with Sheri and I were getting out of control. Sheri would get violent with me, which meant I was violent back at her. Violence was now a normal part of our relationship.

CHAPTER 9

Break Free From the Severe Damage

Suicide attempt again

One night, after Sheri and I had been fighting again, I took a lot of horse tranquillizer pills and went to sleep for three days. This was my second suicide attempt. At one point during my three-day sleep, I woke up and heard some guys in the house talking about what dumpster to throw me in if I died.

The last suicide attempt never prevented me from drinking more and more. Sheri was pissed at me for bringing home booze one night and no weed for her. The fight was on. I was trying to leave the house, but she wouldn't let me. We got physical. I know I pushed her out of the way, and she fell down. She also got clumps of my hair in the altercation.

Third suicide attempt

I went to my mom's house, slept in the basement, and decided to slice my wrist. This was my third suicide attempt. I even felt like a loser trying to kill myself, as I was unsuccessful at this, too. What a loser.

I tried staying with my mom for a while, but Bill, my mom's boyfriend, tried to play the dad role, and I came unglued on him. I said, "If you ever try this again, I will ball bat you, so you should learn your place in this household."

My mom said Bill was scared of me, and I said to her, "He should be. If he screws you around or talks to me like that again, there will be problems."

I heard Sheri's sister had a bunch of guys from the Parkdale crew looking for me to beat the shit out of me. I was so spun and didn't care about my life at that point. I went to the bar they hung out at to settle it so they could decide whether to kill me or leave me alone. I wish they would have killed me.

I was still on parole and not supposed to be drinking, but I was unable to work anymore because work interfered with getting loaded.

The bars I hung out at were the kind where you saw bouncers tie a guy to a chair and beat them.

Break Free From the Severe Damage

Not sure where I was getting my money from to keep drinking, but I was drinking all the time.

I was out at a bar one night, and I got into a fight with this guy. The bouncers arranged for me to continue to beat on this guy in the back alley. I woke up in the morning in the Barton Street bucket again, not knowing what I was there for.

At the courthouse, my lawyer informed me that I was in for a robbery with violence. Since I was still on parole for armed robbery, this offence would get me seven years back in jail.

Spiralling

My mom bailed me out, and my sentencing came six months later. During this time, I couldn't stay sober, and my life spiralled. I knew I would be in and out of jail for the rest of my life. My mom was begging me to stop drinking. I think for the first time, I was honest and said I couldn't.

At my court appearance, my lawyer pleaded me down to an assault with a weapon. I got 13 months in the Guelph Reformatory.

This time, the reformatory was different. This time, I had an attitude. I didn't give a fuck. I was committed to an understanding that this was going to be my life for the rest of my life.

Before I went in, I was framing houses for people who paid cash. They were at the top of the drug chain in Hamilton. When I got in, the eldest brother of the crew I worked for was there.

We became friends and worked in the kitchen. We made homebrews all the time and got drunk at least once a week. He was the man with the dope. He had years in jail, so he knew all the ins and outs of getting the dope I wanted.

We almost got busted with drugs on the inside. My quick thinking got us out of it. I ran across the beds in our dorm and flushed what was in my hands down the toilet, and the other guy hid the dope that he had. My jail buddy was getting out before me, and he made sure I knew how to get a hold of him when I finally got out, as he wanted me to work for him again.

Phyllis aka mom

The reformatory had A.A. meetings, and I went for coffee and donuts. I went so it would look good, not for any other reason.

At one of the meetings, Martin, my ex-sponsor, came in as a speaker. I remember he laughed at me and wouldn't talk to me. On the path I was on, he knew I would end up there. He was right.

Phyllis came in to do an A.A. speaker meeting. I remember Phyllis from meetings on the street. She was a crazy old lady that was off her rocker. However, when she talked and shared her experience, strength, and hopes, she wasn't as crazy as I remembered.

A.A. might be what I need

Maybe this A.A. program had something that I needed. So, I attended more meetings, listened, and decided to give it another try.

My 13-month stint was coming to an end. I was thinking about where I could stash the personal items I had in jail so when (and at that

Break Free From the Severe Damage

point—it was when) I returned to jail, I would be set and comfortable with the things I liked.

Phyllis had planted a seed in me that things could be different, though. I went back to Hamilton and lived at my mom's house. I bounced around to different jobs and took work wherever I could. Jobs were a little hard to come by, but I persisted.

A friend I worked with some time ago, Ed, was doing well with his business framing houses. He wanted me to run his crew for the business, so I said I would need a car. So, we went and got a car. I couldn't afford a licence plate or insurance, so I stole a plate and drove it uninsured.

I was driving my uninsured car with the stolen licence plate to Buffalo, New York, taking my friends to A.A. meetings. It wasn't all that far away from where I lived in Canada. I hung out with a bunch of good people from A.A. but still needed money, so I was quietly selling weed on the side to get it. Although I wasn't smoking it, I felt guilty about this, but I had to do it to get by. That's all I knew.

I had met a good friend, Marlene, through A.A., and she was really helping me to stay on the sobriety path. Marlene asked me to drop her and her sponsee off at Sheree's house.

Sheree was a cute blond who had been around for years and found staying sober a real challenge. Sheree invited me up, and my only thought was, *you want a guy like me in your apartment? I'm too ugly and not worthy of such a beautiful woman.*

My Perfect Storm

Drunk again

Sometime later, I was drinking and went up to her apartment. Sheree was on a bender as well. We drank together, so I relapsed with her. We had fun and drank. She sat on my lap and sang *Kokomo* by The Beach Boys. "Fuckin' drunk again."

I left Sheree's drunk and drove over to my buddy Lenny's house. Of course, I drank more there. I left Lenny's and got pulled over. I was taken in and charged with impaired driving. They impounded my car and let me go. I went back to my mom's house, drank more, and sat on the kitchen floor until I passed out.

Brian, my sponsor from A.A., woke me up, dragged me up the stairs, and threw me in the shower, still in my clothes. I just wanted to go to sleep. He wouldn't let me. He dragged me to an A.A. meeting at noon, then to get coffee and a night meeting. I spent most of the night in the bathroom, throwing up. We went for a coffee after the meeting too.

Sheree was dead

Chris, an A.A. buddy, came to the after-meeting coffee shop and let us know that Sheree had died the night before.

This really destroyed me. I ran down the street for a bit, and they chased me. I punched telephone poles and busted my knuckles up. I could've helped Sheree if I hadn't been drunk. I fucked-up again.

Sheree had just got her daughter back in her life, and now she was dead. Life sucked, and I was mad at myself for not being there for her. Sheree's death was a first for me. Someone who I cared about just died.

Break Free From the Severe Damage

I just wanted to drink, but I didn't. I committed to going to meetings.

My mom and I fought all the time, and I was constantly telling her to fuck-off. I would come home from work thinking, *I'm getting drunk tonight*. Warren or Derrick would be at my house waiting to take me to a meeting. They really looked after me. I guess I appreciated that someone cared, but at the same time thought, *ahh fuck, not them again*.

Marlene kept saying she had a room if I needed it. After telling my mom to fuck-off again, I ended up there one night, and she took me in, giving me a break from mom's house.

CHAPTER 10

The High Waters Seemed to Be Falling

One year sober

I was working in the vegetable section of a grocery store, making minimum wage for the first time ever. The people in A.A. helped me achieve more self-esteem than I ever had. I was one year sober, and I was so proud.

My Perfect Storm

I actually enjoyed going to work even though I was still broke all the time. There was no yelling and screaming like construction work, and I was persevering.

A few people from the local A.A. group and I went to Kingston to an institutional A.A. conference. About 1,000 or so people were there.

I ran into Punchy Proctor. Punchy ran the meeting in Guelph Reformatory. He asked me to read the 12 steps as part of the institutional panel. I agreed to his request and went to take a nap in our hotel room. I woke up saying, "Oh fuck!"

I had done this sort of thing before, just not in front of 1,000 people. There was some fear of getting up on a stage in front of 1,000 people, but I did it.

Martin had become my sponsor. I still felt like I was struggling to stay sober, so I went to an in-house treatment facility not too far from me and was gone for a month. I was making some good friends at this point, and I was a little worried about being in treatment and losing those friendships. I wanted to go see them, but when I enquired about leaving treatment for the weekend, I was told I wasn't allowed. So, like usual, I didn't listen and went anyway.

Navigating being sober and having real feelings and emotions was a new challenge for me. Not being able to just drug or drink them away was something new I was learning.

I needed to get back to work. My brother Ted called and offered me a job. He was living in Maple Ridge, British Columbia. I talked to Martin and decided to leave Hamilton, Ontario, and head to Maple Ridge.

The High Waters Seemed to Be Falling

Working for Ted and living with him and his family didn't last long. I was still in a state where life sucked, things were too hard, and I was angry all the time.

Melinda

Shortly after arriving in B.C., I attended some A.A. meetings again and met a beautiful girl named Melinda. Up to this point, I had never felt worthy of having a girl in my life. At that point in my life, I thought I had fallen in love with Melinda. Now, in retrospect, it really was just lust, but we moved in together.

At work, I was using a Hilti gun that shoots nails through wood into concrete or steel. I was on a ladder stretched out, using it with one hand, when I felt a pop in my wrist. I had pulled the ligaments in my wrist.

I found out Melinda was lying to me all along. She told me that she had split up with her husband for a year, and it actually had only been a few months. So we split up. My inner voice was starting to say, "You are hurt, living in fear, not love, and everyone lies."

I decided I needed a drink. I drank for one day and made such an ass of myself. It was on the day of Melinda's sober-cake acknowledgment at an A.A. meeting, and, of course, I caused a scene.

When I attended meetings after Melinda and I broke up, I felt judged by those who knew her and what I had done. At this point, who could I trust? It felt like all the other A.A. members were her friends, and I was new; I didn't have anyone to really turn to. I made the choice to admit myself to another treatment centre.

Step five

When I went to the treatment centre, I finally worked on my steps for the first time. The A.A. program consists of working through 12 steps to better understand your addiction, clear the wreckage of your past, and open up new choices for your future. I only got to step five during my time at the centre.

I was still very angry and got into arguments all the time.

I even butted heads with Calvin, my assigned case worker, kind of like a counsellor. We had it out after I barged into his office and berated him about how I felt about him; he admitted he felt the same about me. We actually became friends that day.

I guess I was moving forward in some manner as I was now in the Third Stage House, at the treatment centre, which meant a little more flexibility in choices.

I was still angry about getting drunk and wasting a year of sobriety and hard work on myself, but I couldn't let my feelings about Melinda go.

I called mom one day to share my interest in becoming a real estate agent. She told me I couldn't do that. She confirmed all the stuff I couldn't do right, like even just showing up looking like a 'real' real estate agent. At that point, she was right. I really thought I was a loser.

Stone mason

While in the centre, I caught wind of a guy named Cam Wilson who called looking for someone who would take a job as a stonemason's helper. Cam was in Narcotics Anonymous (a similar program to A.A. with a focus on drug addiction).

Stonemasonry was hard work as I usually worked six days a week. Cam demanded you give everything; however, he would stop by every day to talk about recovery, take me for dinners, and introduce me to his friends in recovery.

Chores

At the treatment centre, I was assigned chores. The staff gave me a chore that I had to do every day when I got home from my masonry job. When I came home one day, there was a note on my bed saying the next time my chore wasn't done, I would get a demerit. If I got three demerits, I would be kicked out.

So, as usual, after work, I did my chore, showered, and was off to a meeting.

At the meeting, Billy, the owner of the treatment centre, asked me if I had gotten his note. I said I had and said I did the chore, as usual, when I returned from work. I found Billy was on a bit of an ego trip, and he expected me to get my chore done when he wanted it done. He told me I would get a demerit the next time. I told him to shove it and said, "Then I'm out at the end of the month."

Well, to teach him, I never did any more chores again.

I didn't want to be ripped off by Billy and not get my damage deposit back. So, I made sure he had a clear understanding that I would come after him if I didn't get my money back by the end of the month. This was a normal transaction in my world.

My Perfect Storm

Ironically, I found out my counsellor Calvin was looking for a roommate, so I moved in with him.

It was great. Living together, Calvin and I saw just enough of each other. Calvin went to A.A., and now I was going to N.A. We never saw each other much, but the living arrangements were fine. I was there for about 18 months. I threw myself into N.A. meetings and work.

During my time in N.A., I got Drew as a sponsor (Drool was his nickname). He was around 18 years clean, and I think at that time in my life, and for my age, he was a good fit. Drew and I even ended up working together for Cam.

I went home for a visit, and my 13-year-old niece Katie wouldn't talk to me. She stopped talking to me because I abandoned her when I left Ontario, or at least that's what I was told. Making trips home was always stressful for me, and I often chose not to do them to save my sanity.

Then Calvin moved out, and I got a new roommate who had just split up with his wife.

Clean and still unhappy

I was still angry and lonely. All that seemed to be consistent in my life was the thought—*what's wrong with me?* This was the longest I had stayed at a place for years, and this time, I was clean longer than I had ever been. Even though I had a more stable place to live and had all this clean time, I was still unhappy and working the grind.

I was still hurting from the split up with Melinda. I was confused because it was so good when I was with her. When I attended meetings,

The High Waters Seemed to Be Falling

I saw Melinda's husband, John, and he was always glaring at me. I wanted to just punch him in the head. After all, he did come out winning and got Melinda. I was just the loser.

One day at a meeting, we sat down and talked, and he told me that Melinda told him that the only time we had sex, I tied her up and raped her. I laughed and told John this never happened.

Melinda and I actually had a great sex life. John had seen us together, and even he said he didn't think it added up, but he wanted to believe it so I would be the bad guy. What she said didn't add up for him. John and I later became friends.

I was hurt by all the shit that was going around from John talking about me, and I just couldn't lose my temper again. Why does ugly shit always happen to me?

Cam and I would fight all the time when I was learning how to be a stonemason. I was over-passed by new people he hired because I knew less, so I was always stuck as a labourer. I didn't feel like I fit in anywhere. If people only knew who I was.

I stayed single so long that Drew was bugging me to find girls to date. I quit being a stonemason, tired of working for Cam and tired of the grind and went back to framing houses.

I rode my pedal bike to my new job. On one ride to work, I got hit by a car. My back got so fucked-up, I suffered from the pain for about a year, and I struggled for work and money. After that, I learned how to suffer and deal with the pain. My back was never the same.

Shortly after that, I met Sara at a meeting. We hit it off. She was from Ontario. Things were maybe looking up.

My Perfect Storm

I took out my savings and bought a cheap car and, of course, smashed it up in no time. Kids had put a mailbox out on the road, and, of course, with my luck, I hit it.

I had no luck. I just struggled all the time. I was a loser.

Sara and I moved in together and lived with each other for two years. Up until this point, this had been my longest relationship. I don't remember what happened, but we split up. Again, I found myself in a state of anger. Angry that things never worked out for me. I always felt like I was ugly, and no one wanted me.

I started sleeping with a girl from an A.A. meeting who had a boyfriend. We were actually drinking. I ended up fighting with her boyfriend. He caught us, and he hit her, so I beat him up badly (while in and out of a blackout myself). I only remember hitting him four times. However, I was told I would have killed him if the fight had not been broken up.

Down the tube

There went two and a half years down the tube.

Things started to get bad after this. What better thing to do than run away from my problems? That was what I was used to. So, I decided to go back to Toronto for a short trip. I went and drank the whole time.

I stayed at Phyllis' house. She just loved me. Her family welcomed me and treated me great.

I did some odd jobs for Paula, a friend from A.A., to make a few extra bucks.

Well, it was time to go home. I went back home feeling lonely and angry. I started calling Sara, trying to get her back. I stayed drinking for about four months from when I picked up.

I went back to B.C. and moved in with people from recovery. Things went ok, I guess. I still wanted to kill myself for blowing my time again. I was ashamed for not staying clean all while others were showing me love. This wasn't making sense to me.

I was angry all the time, pushing people away. I ended up in another treatment centre, The Last Door. They wanted a six-month commitment, so I stayed.

I was scared. Fucked-up. I just wanted to kill myself.

I worked on changing. At the treatment centre, I attended two N.A. meetings a day, worked on my steps, participated in the centre-run sessions, and made some good friends.

Still got my anger

My aggression caused me lots of trouble in the treatment centre. It was funny, there was another Scott in the house with me, and we butted heads so badly to the point they 'married' us, so we had to do everything together.

Five and a half months after my admission, I started talking about leaving. They did their best to convince me to stay, and, of course, I got mad at them and threw a shampoo bottle at someone, so I got kicked out for violence.

I knew my anger ruled my life. People would always say, "Just control it." All I knew was I didn't know how to.

My Perfect Storm

So, I got out of the treatment centre and moved in with a new friend from N.A., Primo. He was my new sponsor.

There was another guy that got kicked out of the treatment centre. We decided to go to Alberta for work. We ended up working on a forest fire camp. It was easy, long days, and ok money. The isolation was getting to me, so I told him I was heading back to B.C., where I kept paying Primo to keep my room in his house.

Returning to B.C. I had some grub steak (money) so I could start making some choices.

I got a job with Fraser Masonry. It was ok. I remember there was always lots of yelling and screaming at work. That was normal back then. We could never do enough or be good enough. There wasn't much time for me to attend A.A. meetings either.

I worked a lot of long hours. I would go to meetings dirty from work all the time. In my mind, I was proud of this as I worked so hard. I couldn't figure out why people did not want to work as hard. I was also envious of the people who had free time. What a double-edged sword—work to live and have no time for life or fun.

I was becoming an okay stonemason. Things went on for a few years, and I was making some friends.

I was still always angry. Never feeling much love. I kept people away from me with my anger.

I worked six to seven days a week, including holidays, to make other people happy. I never amounted to anything, or so I thought.

I stayed single for a long time for fear of being hurt or hurting them.

The High Waters Seemed to Be Falling

On one of my trips back home to Ontario, I was at my brother Doug's house, meeting his new wife, Tracy. Ted and Lorie were there as well. It was nice to see Doug doing well.

We were hanging out, talking about growing up and the split up of our parents. We started talking about the train set I really liked when I was young. When I left the house, my parents had sold our family home, and I was told that when they sold the house, my train set was left there.

The train set

The next day, I drove with my mom, and she said to me, "Whenever you would like to talk, I'm here."

I was a little perplexed as to what she was talking about, so I responded, "Talk about what?"

She said, "About the train set."

I said, "What about it?"

She informed me that she had it in her basement.

Again, another lie, untruth, manipulation from my mother.

Carmen

I was back in British Columbia working my ass off, doing side work so I could make more and more money. I met Carmen (again, another relationship through N.A). We hit it off.

My Perfect Storm

I found myself with another recovery friend, Keith, and was sharing a house with him. We were good friends.

One of my mom's aunts died in B.C., so mom came to look after things. My friend Rob hung out with her and helped by driving her around to get things done for her aunt's service.

Sometimes, I thought, *why don't others see what I see about my mom?* When mom left, Rob said he thought I had been exaggerating about my mom and the way she treated me. He confirmed what I always thought about my mom and said I wasn't exaggerating. He said, "I saw the moment when either you or your mother came into the room; daggers would start to fly." For once in my life, it was nice that someone else saw what I saw.

Carmen and I went camping with her kids. We were heading down a gravel road, and she wanted to let her dog out to run, so we let it out. The dog ended up running beside the truck, and it ended up under the tires. I was driving. I killed it with her two kids in the truck.

Despite this happening, we felt like things were going okay, so we moved in together. Things were good for a while. I think we were together for two and a half years, with a few breakups during this period.

We went for counselling, and we could talk, but we never worked anything out. We had just bought a townhouse and were trying to have a baby together. She backed out of the idea and concluded she was crazy to think of having a kid with me.

I was angry. I moved out, got paid out for the house, and ran back to Ontario. Again, confirming my life sucked and nothing ever worked out for me. I thought after living in so many houses, I

The High Waters Seemed to Be Falling

finally found a home where I was working hard to make it the best it could be, and now, I was on the outs again of what seemed like a great relationship.

It was okay at first, but soon, I became depressed, lonely, and angry. How could Carmen do this to me?

I hated going to meetings. Never felt like I fit in. I was the fuck-up that couldn't make things work.

My mom was driving me crazy. She was so needy.

I decided to go back to Vancouver. I asked her for help, and like usual, she said no. I stopped talking to her for a lot of years. She helped all my other siblings out and would never help me.

As I was driving west, I stopped at my friend Mike's house in Abbotsford, B.C. Mike and I had become close. He and his family welcomed me. I lived in my camper in their front yard. I was grateful for Mike's support, but all I thought was, *what a loser to go from owning a house to this.*

I was angry and more depressed than ever. I was a complete loser. How could Carmen do this to me? I loved her. I prayed every night that I wouldn't wake up. I just wanted to die and felt like screaming every morning.

I was unable to work at this point in my life. I was a loser and wanted to die.

My Perfect Storm

Arrested again

I decided to go see Carmen. I was so mixed up, insane, and distraught that when I got there, I tried to take her with me. I was arrested for assault and attempted kidnapping. They did a pre-sentence report, and I really felt like that whole situation was so biased.

Again, I was suffering. I really needed someone to care. Someone to give a shit about me. And again, I only found the 'wrong' person who, again, did me wrong.

The person that did the report was this religious guy. So, of course, he recommended going to a religious recovery house. When I said I was willing to go anywhere other than a place with a religious focus, he said I was being argumentative and rebellious. So, I was sentenced to six months for assault. At that point, I was six years clean, and I was in jail for being a loser. Man, I wanted to die.

At that point, I didn't care. Being in jail did feel safer than being on the street.

This is when I learned freedom is an inside job. No one can take freedom away except yourself. I had thrown mine away. They also said I needed to see some doctors. They decided to put me on so many drugs. Drugs for depression and an antipsychotic drug, too. I walked around like a zombie.

After two-thirds of my sentence, I was released. Since I was lonely, I decided to get a dog. This was actually pretty funny when you think of it because I didn't even have a home at the time.

I was looking through the paper one day and spotted an ad that was selling dogs. I went to the location and spotted a cute little Jack Russell puppy. I got her and named her Tymer. If I ever had a son, I wanted to name him Tymer, although, at this point, if I had a child, they would probably need therapy being named after my dog.

Scott's first jack russel dog named Tymer sitting on his bike.

CHAPTER 11

The Fuckin' Rising Temperatures Again

Fucked up again

I was back in town, and my body was so fucked-up. My back was done. Being a stonemason was hard on my body, so I decided to take a work program. I met a girl who was new to recovery. She was hot. We hung out a lot. I was desperate for anything. I was lost, lonely and angry. My family was right; I was supposed to be in and out of jail and amount to nothing.

This 'hot girl' got loaded on crack and got kicked out of the house she stayed in. I felt like I could help her. I got high on crack for the first time with her. That was six and a half years of clean time down the drain. What a fuck-up I was.

Crack is the most insidious drug I have ever used. Thankfully, this only lasted about three weeks. The combination of drugs, lack of control, and living a life of disgust was almost deadly. In the craziness of it all, I almost killed her in a drugged-up situation where I was being too aggressive. Not sure what exactly happened, but I got out of there.

Fourth attempt

I was so ashamed of myself and where I had ended up. I ended up slicing my wrist halfway up, and I didn't bleed, so I took all my prescribed lithium, and I woke up sick three days later. What a loser. I couldn't even kill myself. My fourth attempt at suicide.

I was taken to the hospital to be looked over, but there wasn't much they could do. The doctors didn't keep me. I was scared, lonely, and wanting help, and I decided they didn't care either.

Back home alone. I tried going to meetings but couldn't do it. I didn't belong there anymore. Mike came to see where I was staying, took me back to Abbotsford, and wouldn't let me leave. I guess he kind of kidnapped me. He cared about me and was so worried about me. I stayed there long enough to get on the straight and narrow again with some stability.

All I had left was a beater motorcycle. I lost everything I had built up. Orville, a good friend from N.A., sold me a Harley on a payment plan.

I stayed clean for just over a year. I wasn't going to very many meetings, and then I got hurt at work. I was hanging out with people who smoked weed, and I was in pain. I knew it would take the pain away, so I got high again.

Smoking a joint was great. It took the physical and mental pain away for a few months. I smoked more and more at work, rest and play. I was crying all the time. I didn't even leave my apartment other than for work.

I was terrified of pushing people away and being lonelier, so I learned how to not take my anger out on others as much. Even though I was managing this area, I still found myself going downtown to cash a cheque and find someone who would sell me enough heroin so I could just end it all.

Heroin

I had never used heroin before, and I was going to get enough to kill myself. I sat on a bench in the rain for four hours, contemplating life. I thought a lot about my previous attempts and how I couldn't even do that right.

I eventually got up, put killing myself out of my head, and decided if I didn't have the balls to kill myself, I better get living.

The payments

Orville and his wife Janet split up. After that split, Orville started dating a girl I recently dated. I left his house feeling depressed and lonely. How could he do this to me? We had been friends for so long.

Orville started calling me and harassing me for the money for the Harley payments. He was back using drugs and needed more money even though I was on top of my payments. Of course, even though I thought all was going well with the payments, it ended up as a fuck-up. I ended up crashing my Harley in a ditch, putting a big dent in the gas tank, and losing my windshield. Now, I had to ride around on a Harley with a big dent.

Shitty

I went for a haircut from my friend Lesley (from N.A.). She asked me how I was doing, and I said, "Shitty."

Lesley replied, "You should give back to the program and get some sponsees."

I replied, "I need to get clean first."

Lesley talked me into going to a meeting, so I decided to go that night.

I went to meetings every night for a week and chose to stay clean.

Orville called and left a threatening message on my phone. I was so pissed off I decided to get high. However, this was the last time I used. That night, I went to a meeting high and listened.

At that meeting, Lesley asked how long I had been clean, sarcastically looked at my wrist, and said, "Ah, 30 minutes."

Yes, I told her I was loaded, and she asked if I was embarrassed. I said, "No." I was working out if I wanted to be clean or not.

The Fuckin' Rising Temperatures Again

I didn't know if I wanted to be clean, but this was 2003, and it was the last time I used a substance. Trying to find my reason to live clean was a real struggle for me.

I even got off all my meds. Life was ok, but I was still struggling for meaning and purpose. I kept going to meetings and started to let a few people in.

You see, I felt like I was judged a lot. My anger kept people away. I was so broken I thought I was wasting my time at meetings. I thought and said all the time, *this won't work for me,* and of course, that was the way my life always played out. So why would it work this time?

Mike Perrier walked up to me and said, point-blank, "You're right. It won't work for you, but it will work for millions of others."

With this, he pounded his finger on my chest and walked away. This was a light bulb moment for me, and I decided to conform to the N.A. world. Today, I believe this was one of the big moments that saved my life.

I threw myself into recovery. I did what was suggested and went to lots of meetings. Despite my feelings about getting the 30, 60, and 90 fobs (milestones of recognition in recovery), I got up and received them. Yeah, I was embarrassed and ashamed for having to do this again and again in my life. How could I let myself have accomplishments in my life when I only screwed them up every time. Would this be any different?

Sunstroke

One Friday at work, I got a bad case of sunstroke. I went up to a baseball tournament and was outside all weekend. The next week, I got sick with lots of dizziness or equilibrium problems, and I couldn't work. Since I wasn't physically able to work, I went to lots of meetings and worked the steps. I ended up being off work for about 11 weeks.

I was vigorously honest about clearing all the wreckage from my past. Even all my debt, for the first time.

My anger was the biggest thing standing in my way. It was the only thing left, and my stance was that if people didn't like me or what I was doing, they could just fuck-off. I always felt that if you had my life, you would be angry too.

My past actions in recovery have created a life of pain and misery. I felt like I was judged by people in the rooms of N.A. I felt condemned to living a lonely life. I didn't know how to change this. I always thought it was me or maybe the inbreeding of my family (of course, this was just an inside joke).

Mostly, what I've come to learn in my life is that people stayed away from me, and very few ever really let me in.

The shift

For some reason, I decided I needed to just keep going.

The government was after me for the money I owed them. This time, I took responsibility and cleaned every debt I could find I owed. It took five long years to clear up the financial stuff.

I was starting to notice that I was surrounding myself with great people.

The Fuckin' Rising Temperatures Again

Orville was clean and in a local recovery house, making my life hell. He was spreading stories that I wasn't paying my Harley payments and even sleeping with his wife, which wasn't true.

Janet, his ex, was being supportive and dragged me into her group of friends. She asked me if I would finish paying her for the Harley as Orville wasn't giving her anything. I talked to some friends and decided that I would pay her. This way, I could hold my head high, help her out, and get that debt off my back.

There was a lot of gossip running around about me. It always felt like if people couldn't find something nice to say about me, they would just find something to say about me that usually wasn't true and, most of the time, reflected badly on me.

I discovered that having a Harley and being in recovery was a lot of fun. It opened doors to new possible relationships with women as I was tired of being alone.

I was feeling much better mentally. I was on a better path, even with the 11 weeks of dizziness. Being out of work, I was broke, scraping by and not eating some days. I was too proud to ask for help. I was still feeling depressed, so I went back on antidepressants.

Jill

I felt like I tried to do things differently. I did my best to continue dating from the day I got clean. My sponsor, Jason, often bugged me to stay single. I just kept telling him I was trying things differently this time. I dated Jill for a while and really liked her, but she dumped me. Looking back, I believe I was too toxic for her anyway. I don't blame her; however, I did stay clean for the first time after dating someone.

The next summer, the dizziness came back for about eight weeks. I had gone to the doctor, but they weren't much help. At the hospital, they thought I was attempting to get drugs from them. So again, they did not want to help.

Andrea

I met Andrea. We dated for a year or so. Just as I was feeling really committed to the relationship, it started to get toxic. It was like… here we go again.

I broke up with Andrea, but I chose to stay clean again.

Relationships never seemed to work out for me. I still had so much anger inside, but I continued to stay clean the whole time.

I finally promised myself that every girl I dated would be treated better than the last, and I would learn from my shortcomings.

I continued to attend meetings, and I continued to get judged by the guys at the local recovery house. They made things harder for me from the gossip they heard about me. I felt like no matter how many meetings I attended, no matter what I strived to be better at, I always found my past was never going to let me break free and move forward.

I was renting a basement suite from the guys that went through the treatment centre (The Last Door). One of the guys was a real pain in the ass, always pushing my buttons. When he was complaining about me smoking, there was some talk about getting me kicked out of the suite. I did everything in my power to stay. I wanted to stay on the sober path and not solve problems with my anger. Every time I was pushed, I wanted to push back even harder. That's all I knew.

Mike and Nancy

Mike and Nancy split up. Mike was being a dick towards me, and looking back, I can see he was just angry. Angry about his broken relationship with Nancy, and I was just conveniently there.

Finding some solace

I did find some solace in my life. My amazing dog Tymer went everywhere with me. She even rode on my lap on my Harley. She was a good buffer between me and other people.

I became close friends with my friend Colleen and her husband, Mike. We often rode together. Over the years, Colleen had attempted to help me. I always rebuffed her. She was one of those 'Door' people, and I did not like them.

After my experience going through The Door, I felt I was judged a lot, and when I left, I had no support from the people I thought were my friends. In the end, I decided I wanted nothing to do with them.

I acted out in anger all the time. I was loud, obnoxious, and even pushed others enough to see if I would get a reaction from them. Maybe they'd be aggressive towards me; however, I've never really hit anyone.

My favourite word was 'fuck'. It was to make a point. Keep people away and sound like I didn't give a shit.

I continued working on myself and staying clean. I poured myself into being a great stonemason who worked six to seven days a week.

My Perfect Storm

I got a phone call one day from Andrea. She told me how her 15-year-old son killed himself, so I went out to see her.

Andrea asked me to take her for a ride, so I did. We were out for a little while, and when we got back, I was told I was not welcome there. I guess they all thought I took her out and took advantage of her.

I was feeling shunned again. It spurred my hatred for people just a little more. These people were supposed to be my friends. I felt like I was consistently judged by people. These are friends who once showed they cared for me, and now, they were turning on me. What was confirmed over and over again was that people were full of shit.

I discovered a group of people called the Soberiders. I heard about them at an A.A. meeting. They were a recovery riding group, and they wanted to have fun riding motorcycles while staying sober, of course.

A Soberider A.A. group! This was such a great idea. I was sober, and I wanted to ride. At that point, it seemed like the best idea, as I was having such a hard time with my life.

Shannon

I went to a ball tournament put on by the N.A. chapter, and this is where I met Shannon. I really liked her. She was great-looking and kind and brought me a hot dog during the tournament. I found out she lived in Maple Ridge, so I decided to attend some Maple Ridge meetings to see if I could track her down. When I did, we started dating that summer.

The Fuckin' Rising Temperatures Again

The dizziness came back again. That 'I'm fucked' feeling came back again too. I had a new relationship in my life, and now what? Feeling like crap from the dizziness, I lost my cool with my new landlord.

It was kind of a weird occurrence. When I finally calmed down with the landlord, I twisted my neck; it cracked and relieved the pressure I was feeling that made me dizzy. I knew it was not an inner ear disease like the doctors said it once was.

Riding to Maple Ridge to see Shannon was a hassle, so I decided to move there and rent a basement suite. Shannon kind of just moved in with me and never went home.

Being in Maple Ridge was a nice, clean break from all the crap from where I lived in New Westminster. I got away from all the gossip and crap around the cliquey recovery people.

Shannon was working at Starbucks and was starting university in the fall for criminology. We both got involved with Soberiders and did fun events with them, like the pig roast, an event filled with socializing and games. It was fun. Life seemed to be better.

I was working for a masonry company in downtown Vancouver. On my way to work one day, the city bus I was on got into an accident and I got hurt. I pulled my shoulder. I was off work for the following six weeks. I had a lot of physio appointments.

When I was all healed up, I got the idea to start my own stonemason business. I called it Tymer Stoneworks, after my awesome Jack Russel.

Running my own business felt like I was always chasing work and chasing the next buck. Every day felt like a grind.

My Perfect Storm

I was going to lots of meetings every night and decided I was going to do what it took to never drink again. With what I learned about myself when I drank and my challenges interacting with other people, it was hard for me to work under other people, so running my own business seemed to be the best answer. I knew I was a hard worker, and I always got the job done right.

Enrolling people in my life has not been a strong suit of mine. I did make good money running Tymer Stoneworks and worked so hard that I did a lot of damage to my body.

I always worked where the money was, so I had to travel hours back and forth from work. I started putting more energy into work than recovery. I would go to meetings dirty from work and tired all the time.

Shannon and I lived together for a while in that little basement apartment.

I made a new friend in Maple Ridge, Freddy. He took me under his wing and helped me rebuild my Harley. He got it painted, and it looked amazing.

I was starting to have things in my life to be proud of. I had my business, a new truck, sobriety, friends, food in the fridge, and I was living with a great girl.

Shannon was going to school full-time, and I was working a lot. Unfortunately, that meant I didn't really have a lot of time for me to just have fun. Even with being so busy, Shannon and I seemed to just work things out. Life was pretty great.

Shannon had a big family, and we celebrated lots of holidays together with them. It was a little like being a kid again. Having fun during the holidays.

The Fuckin' Rising Temperatures Again

I was getting some stability and not moving every six months out of a shitty place to another shitty place. After earning her criminology degree, Shannon got a job in the prison system. I didn't like it because, of course, I knew what happened there. I thought she might not be safe there.

My aunt Cathy contacted me and said she wanted to come see me. She came and met Shannon. It was great; we talked a lot about my mom and why I chose not to talk to her.

When Aunt Cathy couldn't persuade me to talk to my mom, Cathy, Shannon, and I decided I would write my mom a letter explaining why I didn't talk to her anymore.

We spent months emailing back and forth about what this letter should include. They helped me write a letter that was to the point and not too mean.

My Perfect Storm

I decided to buy Shannon a ring. I asked her mom first if I could have her hand in marriage and then asked Shannon to marry me. When I went down on one knee to ask her to marry me, she called me a dork. I continued on, though, and she said yes. Life was coming together.

We started looking for a bigger place to rent. I was a little annoyed because the rent was so insanely expensive. We wanted to rent a main floor of a house that had a garage so I could store my bike and tools from work.

We were so turned off by throwing money away in rent that we decided to buy a place instead. We started looking, and somehow, we bought a house with Shannon's mother and her mother's boyfriend, Ken. Things were working out. I had a family in my life.

I finally got myself out of old debt and felt like I could be something! Dare I be excited for my life?

Things started to go sour when we were building a basement suite for Shannon and I on the lower level of the house. We had one of Ken's friends doing the kitchen cabinets. He would tell us what we wanted to hear and then go up and tell Ken and Marion something different. This caused lots of problems. Ken and I almost had a fistfight over it.

We all stopped talking over this miscommunication about the renovation. It made for a pretty intense situation. We ended up buying them out. Shannon's relationship with her mom never improved until she split up with Ken.

During this time, Shannon and I supported each other with all this shit going on. We kept working on the house and living life.

The Fuckin' Rising Temperatures Again

It got to the point that every six months, Shannon and I would have a big fight and stop talking. That's how our whole relationship seemed to be. Things would be ok, and then there were major times of not talking at all. I never knew where I stood in our relationship. This was my life. I never knew where I stood with people.

Mexico

Colleen and Michael moved to Mexico. Shannon and I would go see them.

On one occasion, I went down to Mexico by myself. When I was down there, I was unsure if I wanted to be married to Shannon anymore.

So when I went home, Shannon and I had a big fight, and I left to go back to Mexico. I stayed there for a month and a half this time. I did a set of steps (through the A.A. program) with Colleen (as she was well-versed in the steps), and I took this time to learn how to scuba dive.

It was a great trip; however, it was filled with both fun and stress. Of course, the stress of wondering what to do in my life in regard to my marriage to Shannon.

Of course

On my way home, I was pulled into customs. Of course, I was. I had my little Jack Russell, Tymer, with me, and I was sporting an ear infection from all the diving I was doing in Mexico. Getting 'jacked-up' at the airport was the last thing I needed.

My Perfect Storm

It was a bit of a pain in the ass. I was accused of interfering with an investigation of my bags as they so nonchalantly threw them around and really didn't care about my stuff. They arrested me, and I was so pissed.

I demanded the video of what went down with their request to look through my bags, and I added that I would let the media know about the crappy way I was treated and how the officer literally threw my luggage around. Well, I was on my way shortly after that, and they probably realized I was too much of a pain in the ass.

When I went home, Shannon was seeing a counsellor and asked me if I would go. I had decided that our marriage was worth working on, and I wasn't willing to give up yet, so I went.

We were going to this marriage counsellor, and it seemed like we talked a big game and went through the motions; however, we had already tried a therapist and knew our relationship wasn't improving.

I felt Shannon was a lot like my own mom. She complained about a lot of stuff, like my smoking and the fact that I liked riding too fast.

I came to realize I was also like my dad and how he acted with my mom. My mom got whatever she wanted, and when dad wanted something, it always meant an argument. Shannon and I fought about everything. It seemed, like my parents, Shannon got what she wanted, and when I wanted something, we had big fights and arguments.

We seemed to have an 'ok' marriage at times. I was busy doing my work and doing renovations in our house. Shannon and I were making things work and having a little fun. We did love each other.

The Fuckin' Rising Temperatures Again

I got this big job doing stonework. The owner, Al, said he was sober, but he smoked weed. Most of the guys on the job smoked tons of weed as well. I became friends with Al and then became his A.A. sponsor.

Lynn

Al rode a Harley as well and was a little crazy like me. He was older than us, and Shannon and his wife Lynn got along well. We went for a bike ride together and took in an A.A. Round-Up in Kamloops for the weekend. It was great.

On the way home from the Round-Up, there were about seven riders cruising together. I was leading the pack, and Al was right behind me. Al veered off into the ditch, hit a small rock, and the bike was catapulted with Lynn on the back. I saw it all as Al's cry out of 'FUCK' resonated in my ears while Lynn flew through the air.

Lynn hit the rock face cliff, and her limp body bounced and landed back down in front of our group of bikers. Phil ended up riding over Lynn. It was all so fast, and I watched all of it in my sideview mirror. It was horrific.

I wanted to spare Shannon from the scene, so I told her to walk away from what had just happened as she was on the back of my bike. I told her, "You go that way."

I quickly went to Lynn and did my best to comfort her and see if there was anything I could do. From what I saw, there was little to be done. Lynn was bleeding from her mouth. She wasn't responsive or really breathing. Al was calling out for Lynn. We told him to stay where he was as he was hurt, too.

My Perfect Storm

It was hours before paramedics arrived. They looked her over and said there was nothing they could do either. Lynn was gone.

I think I was in shock that day. Not sure what to think.

Al, who had broken his collarbone, was rushed to the hospital in Merritt. We all went to Merritt before he was transferred to Kamloops. All the riders that were there went up to the Kamloops Hospital.

A buddy, Mike Greaves, drove up from Vancouver in his truck to haul Phil's crashed bike away and be there for us. The riders in Kamloops got together at a local Denny's, which stayed open later for us. Most of the people from that night have been in and out of my life since then. There were about 25 of us supporting each other. It made me feel loved, and I wasn't used to this.

A new buddy I just met, Mike Laramee, put his keys for his truck in my hands and said, "We think you should park your bike and take my truck." This kind of loving gesture was different for me. It was a different feeling.

This crash and having Lynn die in my arms really affected me. It changed how I approached other traumatic experiences in my life. When I was out biking or driving later, I would go into a sense of shock if I saw an accident. It was always not far from my brain. I had a hard time processing that fatal event and moving past it.

Shannon and I continued to be involved with Soberiders and the pig roast events. Mike Laramee and I became good friends.

I met another new friend, Jenn, who was Mike's girlfriend at the time. Mike and Jenn were great to hang around with in Kamloops.

CHAPTER 12

Some Clearing in the Shit Storm

Sweat ceremony

Three years after the accident, Gord, my brother Gary's ex-wife, had a native sweat lodge on her property. Just before attending the sweat lodge, Andrew, a fellow friend, had accidentally killed a kitten Shannon and I had. The kitten was under our rocking Lazy Boy chair when Andrew was on it. He didn't realize the cat was under there when he was rocking it, and the kitten was killed. I was the first one to see the cat dead.

My Perfect Storm

The sweat ceremony was a ritual of purification in this dome-shaped structure where you pray to the grandfathers and grandmothers. So, I was in this sweat ceremony, having visions of my dead kitten's face and then Lynn's face. It got faster and faster, switching back and forth between the two.

Then, in this vision, my grandmother, who died many years ago when I was six, was standing way up on a hill and said to me, "It's all going to be ok." It was strange, and I wasn't sure how much I believed in that stuff; however, it was healing.

I did start to notice the pain around Lynn's death began to subside after this sweat lodge experience.

Shannon and I continued to struggle in almost every area. We wanted different things with no tools in our toolboxes to fix our marriage. We were stuck in our own traumas from the past. Having a sexless marriage was hard, and I feel we were just afraid to let go.

For me, I was too afraid of losing things again. I didn't think I would recover mentally, so I just stayed.

After Lynn died, Shannon decided to get her bike licence. I was proud of her. She worked through her fears and did it. She rode my old Dyna. We rode all the time and put miles behind us. Even on our holidays, we would rent Harleys and go riding.

One summer, we took a long bike trip. On the first day of our trip, I decided to quit smoking. Shannon had been bitching at me for years to quit, and finally, I chose to quit, and she wasn't very supportive. She was pissed at me, and all she could say was, "You're going to quit on our holidays?" This was the crappy dynamic in our relationship.

Some Clearing in the Shit Storm

About six months after I stopped smoking, I got really sick with a lung infection. After four days of feeling like crap with this lung infection, I still thought of Shannon and how I could show up for her. I made sure to heat up the house with a warm fire in our fireplace. I wanted the house to be warm when she came home from work, but she overlooked my efforts and instead found the one thing that pissed her off. She noticed my shoes weren't on the doormat and got really pissy at me. On that day, I decided I was done with Shannon. I guess it was a matter of time.

Closing Tymer Stoneworks

At that point in our marriage, I was just putting my time in, hoping we could pay the debt down so we could walk away with something. However, I got tired of always making things work. I felt like I was gambling with every job. Hiring people was a nightmare. I was too hard on them. They didn't stay. I decided to shut down my stonemason business and returned to work under other people again.

We thought we'd give it another try and started seeing the counsellor every other week. I felt like I had given everything I had and had nothing left to give. We were at the point where Shannon didn't even want me to drive. I had given up control of the money and the household stuff, but nothing I did was good enough anyway.

Shannon decided she wanted a baby. We tried for a bit. It felt like the only reason she wanted sex was just to have a kid. Our counsellor even told me not to get her pregnant.

My friends, Andrew and Elissa, moved to Maple Ridge and Shannon and I became good friends with them. We rode together, hung out and had some fun times. It was great.

My Perfect Storm

One day, Shannon told my buddy, Mike Greaves' girl Nancy, that she didn't like her, so Mike stopped talking to me. Things like this really reinforced that I was a loser. I felt like I didn't want to live anymore, and I was too angry to attract any good people in my life. I also worked too much.

Life was just a grind. Wherever I went, bullshit happened.

I worked the steps and could never figure out how I attracted so much bullshit. I couldn't even keep friends or let anyone into my life. It was too painful.

Shannon and I lived a lonely life in our house. We were pretty much just roommates who shared a room and would mask it by showing people how good we were by having Christmas parties and BBQs at our house.

We were going to the counsellor all the time, and one day, Shannon said she wanted a separation. My reply to this was, "Then get the fuck out of my house."

She made plans to move, then said she was staying to protect her investment. I lost my shit, yelled and screamed, convinced her to move, and changed the locks. I ended up keeping the house. Of course, we later divorced.

I had to do a little scamming with paperwork to get the house. This was another nightmare I got myself into. I was going to meetings depressed, feeling judged by the people who I thought were my friends, but they turned out to be Shannon's friends, not ours. I was angry that my phone didn't ring, and I became resentful and bitter. I went to different meeting groups to hopefully meet some different people. However, angry Scott just showed up.

Some Clearing in the Shit Storm

The weekend Shannon moved out, I bought a new 2015 Harley Road Glide and a dirt bike. I decided to rent out rooms in my house, which was a nightmare. It was mostly people from recovery. I would kick them out, and they would bash my reputation to others, and this pushed me further out of wanting to go to A.A.

I got violent with one guy. He called the cops. What a pain in the ass.

I was so angry that I didn't fit anywhere. A recovery friend, Andrew Kidd, and I had some words, and our friendship was done. I was a fuck-up. I wasn't sure why I even stayed clean. I was so toxic to people who once cared for me. I'm sure they cringed when I called them.

At this point, I was having severe bouts of depression and suicidal thoughts, even though I was taking antidepressants. My work was all over the map. I was a failure.

Working in Alberta

I was working in West Vancouver, and traffic was hell going to and from work. It was getting worse day by day. There was one week where, three out of five day days, it took me five hours to get home each time because the traffic was so bad. The stonemasonry work and commuting were getting to be too much. The traffic was slowly killing me.

I started taking courses that were needed to work in the oilfields in Alberta. I got my First Aid certificate and completed the Hydrogen Sulfide (H2S) training course, too. I took my Level 3 First Aid and moved on to become a licensed emergency medical responder. Having just been split up with Shannon, I eventually got a job in Fort McMurray, Alberta and was hired as an emergency medical responder (EMR).

My Perfect Storm

Life was scary. I was now doing new stuff and wondering where the hell I would end up.

After a few shifts as an EMR, I looked around and decided to get my class one licence to drive rigs for the oil fields.

I ended my EMR position as driving rigs was way more attractive to me. My first job driving was with a family-run company. It was crazy, and I was always nervous about going to my new job because I wasn't used to being the guy who knew nothing.

There were a lot of assholes; I found them, and they found me. I was in conflict a lot and then ended up spitting in this guy's face, so I was let go.

I got hired at another job, and they had a guy that liked to yell at me. Well, I stopped the truck one day and wanted him to get out to fight, and he wouldn't, so he complained to the boss that I had threatened him. We had a meeting, and I told the boss and him the truth. I told him if he yelled at me one more time, I was going to end up in a fight with him, and that was that.

It really annoys me that I encounter people all the time who want to cause problems, but when you bite back, they run to their bosses. Well, that job ended shortly after this, and I was looking for work once again.

I decided to put my house up for sale and move to the island, where I could pay cash for a house. Then, I could start to take it easy and enjoy life.

A friend, Robert Stanhope, aka Big Daddy, called and got me a job driving for the Teamsters in the movie business. It was great pay and long hours. It kept me busy and away from the crap I often dealt with in my world.

Fucked up house sale too

I finally had buyers for my house after it was on the market for about three months. I settled a contract to sell my Maple Ridge house, but, of course, nothing was easy in my life, and the prospective buyers bailed on the deal five hours to move in time. What a nightmare! I couldn't even sell my house.

The real estate agent I hired was a piece of work, too. Again, I was stuck in a position where I felt I had to push my weight around to get things to go my way. I was stuck with the house at this point.

This house had lots of bad memories, so here was one more thing to add to the list of things that sucked in my life, from a f'd up family to divorce to a very long list of things I struggled with constantly. It took almost two years to settle with the people who were going to buy my house, and it still cost me money.

CHAPTER 13

Major Forces of Disruption

Dr. Amen

I met a guy named Steve from the Teamster's job. He had been sober for 20 years and relapsed. Steve wanted to go back to meetings. We started hanging out together. I was taking him to meetings. One day, he came up to my truck at work and put a book from Dr. Amen in my hand.

When Steve gave it to me, he said, "You might find it interesting because it might explain why you are the way you are."

When I read the book, it was all about head injuries and ADD (Attention Deficit Disorder). Dr. Amen had a clinic in the United States, and at this point, I couldn't afford to go see him and inquire about my own head injuries or even travel to the states.

Life still sucks

Things were good for a while. Then as time went along, the angry, asshole Scott showed up again, so I was having a hard time getting along with people. This was a big thing for me, as well as not being able to keep my mouth shut.

I always had to stick up for what I felt was the right thing. Like always, I became known as the troublemaker for some reason. I was judged harshly by others. It's been like this my whole life.

I started to realize I had become the victim like I said I never wanted to be. However, I had no idea how to change. In this movie business job, I realized that I was a neanderthal. I just accepted this and knew I would try and fit in; however, my mouth and triggers wouldn't let me.

My one friend told me I acted like people were out to get me. I wasn't sold on this. I just felt like I got judged too harshly by people. Today, I see that my energy was a drain on others.

For me, life seemed to be a constant state of asking myself *why*. Why did I find myself in situations that seemed to destroy any hope of moving forward?

Major Forces of Disruption

More bullshit

I was out one day riding with some friends, and a fellow rider, Kelly, wiped her bike out. To make a long story short, she ended up suing me. She, along with Janet and another guy, backed up her story even though this lie was total bullshit. I was found responsible.

This just made me hate people more. I started to feel like I didn't have much use for people. I was broken and defeated, almost begging for help from people, not knowing what to do. I just stumbled along with little to no hope. I would continue to ask the same people for help or do the same thing to get healthy, but nothing worked.

I found that in every Teamster show I worked on, there was a conflict. I would get a new show and think, *this time will be different,* and it never was. I just felt cursed, like the universe hated me. It didn't matter what I did; things would never change.

The 'C' word

After reading Dr. Amen's book, I decided to go to G.F. Strong (a head and back clinic) to get some info on head injuries and maybe a little insight into myself. In order to get a referral for this clinic, I had to get myself a family doctor, so I started with a new doctor.

His protocol was to start with a physical. After the physical, some test results came in. The doctor called me and said I needed to come in to go over the results.

I found out I couldn't go to G.F. Strong because I lived in the wrong area. He said there was a notice in the tests to say my PSA levels were high and that I needed to be referred to a specialist to clarify what was going on.

Within two weeks of that test, my PSA counts were retested. Two days later, the specialist called late one Friday night. I was still at work. I was informed I had prostate cancer, and my counts had gone up two points. I was appreciative I got the news via the phone, but I was surprised she sprung the news on me without really verifying if it was a good time.

This was the ultimate sign that really fucked me up. It was a confirmation that I was a loser and didn't belong in this world. Yes, the universe hates me.

I went for an appointment to find out what I had to do. I was against chemo. The outlook looked grim. I was 50, not even wanting to live. I decided that I was going to let the cancer have its way with me.

Helping Matthew

At the time, my nephew Matthew, Doug's son, started to contact me. Matthew was using meth and wanted to get clean. We talked about him moving in with me. I laid out the ground rules. Staying clean and going to meetings was a must.

Shaun, a guy who rented a room from me, took him under his wing, and I helped Matthew get a job. After six or so months of living clean at my house, Matthew had gotten high, so I had to ask him to leave.

Tara

My niece Tara was also living in Maple Ridge with her brother Craig, and she was going to A.A. meetings. I no longer went to meetings; however, I knew Tara and Matthew needed someone in my family who was living a clean lifestyle and attempting to change.

Major Forces of Disruption

So here I was, 50, and divorced from a sexless marriage with this prostate cancer news. I was now not going to be able to have sex anymore. FUCK. I was angry. My life was fucked. I didn't want to be here anymore.

At this point, I had pushed everyone out of my life with my anger and toxic behaviour. I was living a lonely life, and no one cared about me anymore. If they did try to get close to me, I pushed them away with my negativity. If I did talk to someone, I would just vent about myself and be all negative, keeping them away.

Shit again

Work was fucked. Not fitting in continued to be my life. I would just get comfortable, and shit would happen again.

I wasn't getting much interaction with old friends or new friends. I would have people over to play games but not receive an invite from anyone else to go out. This hurt. I was fucked. No one was ever there for me. I felt all alone.

Fuckin' sucks

At this point, I was so frustrated that I didn't even know what to say. Within three months of my cancer diagnosis, I had a radical prostatectomy, which is cutting my prostate out.

I was told I might have some incontinence; however, I didn't just have some. I was peeing myself all the time. I had to wear diapers, and the pads stunk really bad. I could smell stale urine all the time. I was going crazy.

When I wasn't working all the time, I just stayed at home. I thought I finally got in with a good crew at work. There was one senior member that didn't like me, so he just rode my back all the time. It always seemed like he was trying to get me fired. I worked so hard at showing him I was not the person he thought I was.

The universe hates me

I just wanted to die or get loaded. I was stuck. It didn't matter how I lived; I still never fit in. People just lied to get what they wanted, even doctors. *The universe hates me* is what I always thought and was shown all the time. From peeing my pants to not getting a hard-on.

I would try to go to meetings every now and then and would just be angry, so I couldn't go.

The Basic

My friend, Keith, was telling me about this program called Landmark Forum. I decided to call him about possibly doing it to support my recovery journey. When I talked to him in desperation, he told me there was another program that he actually liked better called PSI, and he got me a cheaper ticket to go. I begrudgingly went as now I found myself having to pay for help.

I took the three-day course and thought the info was similar to the 12-step work. It made sense to me; however, I was able to get something from it. One thing I saw in myself was that I was still in situations where I had a hard time dealing with others and their need to have control was challenging for me.

At the end of the course, I went out on my motorcycle, frustrated that they were doing their best to upsell me to the next course level of help. I was about to put my leg over my Harley and stopped in my tracks. I noted to myself that I would have no problem putting $5,000 into my motorcycle but wouldn't put that into myself. I thought, *I want to put a gun in my mouth, but I won't go for help.* So, I went back in and bought the next course.

Mushrooms

I started researching magic mushrooms hoping for a mental shift. It scared me a lot to think about taking them. I thought if I took them, it would kick my addiction into high gear again.

Philippines

Having a criminal record, I couldn't go to the United States unless I got a waiver. I decided to get it to go to see Aunt Cathy, maybe go to Dr Amen's clinic, and travel. I had put it off for so many years. They made my first waiver for five years, so I decided to go to the Philippines for Christmas break.

I had fun diving every day in the Philippines, but I still felt lonely and embarrassed. My wetsuit smelled like stale urine from me peeing in it. I was still wearing diapers and pads to stay dry. I was by myself, and no one wanted to be with me, and because of all this, I felt like a loser.

Still, when I was diving in the Philippines, I felt some peace. There was some sense of calm and no stress when I was under the water.

Destroyed

The doctor had given me a prescription for the drug that I had to inject into my penis to get it hard. The fact that I had to do this just beat me up more, and I felt like my masculinity was destroyed. There's no way to describe the humiliation of this. I was with one girl there, and it was embarrassing. Everything sucked about me. I was all alone and always would be.

On the fifth day of my trip, I got into an accident on a scooter. I broke my collarbone and had another head injury. This was painful. It was a struggle getting back to the airport.

When I tried to change my ticket, they wanted a 'fit to fly' note from a doctor. It was New Years, so nothing was open. I was by myself in Manila in so much pain.

All I could think was, *fuck I can't even have a holiday. What a fucken' loser. The universe hates me.*

I had to find a button-up shirt to wear as I had this big sling on around my arm and collarbone. All I had were t-shirts that I couldn't get over my head. It was a painful walk to get to the store.

I ended up going to the Canadian consulate in the Philippines. They didn't want to help me. So, I sat down on the property and insisted they either help me or arrest me. They made some phone calls and figured out where I could go for help.

I finally made it back to Canada, and I was in so much pain. It was so bad I would almost puke.

Major Forces of Disruption

About a week after the accident, I was back working 16 or more hours a day at my Teamster job. Thank goodness there was little physical labour involved, or I could at least manage to do it.

Things were going well for the first time in a long time with work. There was only one guy I was having problems with, and still, to this day, I don't even know why. However, this was normal in my life.

I seemed to attract problems, and this would never change because the universe hated me. I was always stressed about work and keeping things together. I stayed busy going from one show to the next.

Covid

So, just as I was clearing myself of debt, Covid hit, and things shut down. I went and got a job driving, and I liked it. I was hauling water out of the Nestle plant in Hope, British Columbia. I was getting insanely angry all the time. I thought I was losing my mind, and I would lose my shit on people and would think, *where did that come from?*

I was drinking water like a mad alcoholic. I was drinking two litres of water overnight while I was in bed. I was making dumb mistakes at work. I had to go pee all the time. I was talking to the doctor about what was going on, and he said it could be my anti-depressants, so I went cold turkey on my meds. Work started shortchanging me on my checks, too.

Someone suggested I should get checked for diabetes. So, I got tested and sure enough, now I had fucken diabetes. What the fuck? This is why I lived my life on guard for what's next.

My Perfect Storm

So, I was pissing my pants, wasn't able to get a hard-on, and now I couldn't eat junk food. Fuck, fuck, fuck, fuck, fuck. My life fuckin' sucks.

I found out from my doctor on a Tuesday that I had diabetes. It was only on Friday, three days later, that the doctor called me to tell me my sugar levels were so high that I should be in the hospital. So, off I went to the hospital.

It was a bad experience. I was already bitter about the health care industry, and now I felt like I was having another horrific medical experience.

The staff didn't seem to be listening to the doctor's orders when it came to my care, and the lady in the bed next to me cried all the time to her husband on the phone. She complained to him that I was a whiny baby. I lost my shit on her. I signed myself out with orders to take insulin and metformin because my counts were so high.

So, I found myself home alone, scared, just wanting to die or get loaded. This was another confirmation that the universe hated me, and I was done.

Food

At this point, we still had Covid restrictions, and people were talking about how much their lives had changed. Well, mine hadn't really changed as I still spent most of my time with my dogs. However, I reached out to Colleen's daughter, Shannon, who was a dietician, for help with the food I needed to keep my diabetes at bay so I wouldn't have to use drugs from the doctor.

Major Forces of Disruption

Going right?

So, when I talked to the diabetes centre and adjusted my diet, I started crashing with low blood sugars and found myself having to pig out before going to bed at night. I figured the food part out and weaned myself off all the diabetes meds (which, at this point, was insulin and Metformin) within three months. Something seemed to be going right!

Pig Roast

My friend Jen talked me into going to Keremeos, where the pig roast was held, even though it wasn't actually happening because of Covid. I went even though I resented a lot of the people there. I didn't feel like being part of it and felt like a big phoney going there. I knew there would even be people there I didn't want to talk to.

Jen was supportive, and it was nice to ride up together with her. Unfortunately, her bike broke down, and her boyfriend came to get her and the bike, so I was left up there alone.

Monday, I got up early and left, so I didn't have to ride back to Maple Ridge with anyone. I rode up to Merritt. It was so cold going through the mountains, but I was so stubborn. I wouldn't even stop to put a coat on; I was so focused on getting out of there.

I did stop at Starbucks in Merritt. There was a bike in the parking lot. I parked far away from it, got a coffee, and sat by myself. I was feeling antisocial and didn't want anyone around me.

Out of the blue, this voice said, "How are you?"

I grumbled, "Ok."

My Perfect Storm

He asked, "Where are you going?"

I grumbled again, "Vancouver."

He asked me if he could go with me, and I grumbled, "Yes."

Even though I just wanted to tell him to fuck off.

I was riding with this guy and thinking, *what are you doing riding with this geek?* However, at that moment, I didn't know how much this man was going to change my life.

I stopped where Lynn had died in my arms and told him all about it. I just stopped in the middle of the highway.

We continued and stopped at a restaurant in Boston Bar for lunch. For some reason, as broken as I was, I told this man about my life, and he said, "It sounds like you need new friends." I laughed and said, "You think?"

I got to know him a little more and found out his name was Chris.

He confessed he was going to Vancouver to see his trauma therapist, and he raved about her. I told him about my experience with E.M.D.R (Eye Movement Desensitisation and Reprocessing), and he said this lady was amazing. I got her number. We finished our lunch, headed on to Vancouver, and just went on our merry way.

Being as fucked as I felt, I ordered some magic mushroom capsules to try despite my 12-step experience. They worked well and made me feel a little lighter and laugh a little. They were a low dosage, just 100 milligrams. When I ordered more, I decided on a 500-milligram chocolate mushroom, too.

Major Forces of Disruption

Is this considered a relapse?

One Saturday morning, with no food in my stomach, I ate the 500-milligram mushroom-filled chocolate. I got sick, went to bed, and had quite the experience. I had dreams of people I resented and woke up feeling like I had processed my resentments. I felt great, lighter and laughed a little more. However, I felt like I had gotten loaded, and of course, it would be looked upon as losing my clean time, so I was hesitant to tell my friends. I did this for therapy, nothing else. Having grown up in 12-step programs, this was a big challenge for me.

Work started up again, and I had gotten in contact with Kimberly Davidson, the trauma therapist that Chris told me about. She was good. I felt comfortable with her. She confirmed that I didn't get loaded when I told her what I did with the mushrooms. She asked me, "Did they help?" and I told her, "They did."

At this point in my life, I was micro-dosing and feeling like life might be ok. I was laughing more, not thinking of dying all the time.

I was having a session every week with Kimberly on Zoom. At first, I wasn't sure about her or doing it on Zoom, but it was good. I started to trust her, and it was making a difference.

Work was always stressful. I got into it again with a guy at work, and he went to the big boss. Have I ever said I hated rats? You know what I mean? People who rat others out?

Because of this, work got uncomfortable again. I started talking to friends about what I was doing with the mushrooms. Many were skeptical and worried it might throw me back into a life of addiction, but they were seeing a change in me.

My Perfect Storm

I was working fairly steadily, and I was making good money. So far, life was always based on me working and making money, not on whether I was having a good experience.

CHAPTER 14

Comfort from the Storm?

A Dodge Dart

I started searching for a 69 Dodge Dart. I had wanted a Dart since I was a kid, and I never thought I would have one.

I borrowed a trailer and went to Redding, California, to buy one. I drove it back to the Canada/U.S. border. It was a little bit of a pain getting it across the border, but I did it.

My Perfect Storm

These two young guys were recommended to me to rebuild the Dart. Unfortunately, they always had a story about getting the car done, and it seemed like they were screwing me over. If I hadn't changed how I reacted to others, I probably would have beat the living shit out of both of them. They had the car for two years. Things always go sour for me.

At that time, I was working on the offset side of movie production, and this took the stress off me with fewer hours and fewer people to deal with.

There was a close friend who was an advocate for magic mushrooms. John, Mark, and some guy I didn't know came to my house to do a ceremony. I think we did five grams of mushrooms. The experience was great. I laughed and had fun, but nothing major happened other then it made me feel lighter; the problems I had in my life didn't seem as big.

Going into the journey, we talked about our intentions for taking the mushrooms. My intention was to dig deep and figure out where my anger came from. I wanted to understand why I was always messed up. We started with meditating. I had a blindfold on, and I played meditation music.

I had moments where I felt like I did when I was a kid when I was taking this hallucinogenic. I felt how lost I was with no direction in life. Looking back at how lonely and scared I was, I realized I never stood a chance at success. I was only a kid making lots of important decisions when I had no clue how to live life.

After my mushroom journey, I found some forgiveness for myself and the things I had done. The next few weeks were great. I laughed a little more and things were coming together. Today, I see how the mushrooms helped me open up and look at things in a different way.

Comfort from the Storm?

Around the same time, I decided to list my house, blow my life up, and see where I landed, as there were a lot of unhappy memories in this house with my shitty marriage. The day after I listed the house, a rodent chewed the water pipes in the basement and wrecked the drywall ceiling. This was a huge stressor for me.

I finally made the decision to make a shift in my life and again, look at what happened. I really felt like I was cursed. I couldn't even fix the damage myself. I was working every day, and I had tenants, so it needed to be fixed fast. Plus, I was trying to sell it. I was so stressed.

I had an upcoming surgery for a mechanical sphincter to help me stop peeing my pants all the time. The doctor wanted me to stay overnight, but the hospital suggested I go home after my last blow-up when I was in for my diabetes.

So, the morning after the surgery, Bobbie, my tenant, called and said there was another leak in the ceiling. I had no money to pay to fix it and no friends to help. So, I fixed it myself. I was supposed to have my feet up doing nothing and taking time to heal from this surgery, but I had myself working on the leaking ceiling with stitches in my freshly cut-open ball sack and stomach. I was angry and felt sorry for myself.

My friend Jenn was staying with me to help me after my surgery. I was too angry, and she just pushed my buttons even harder. I ended up throwing her out of the house. Fuck there goes one of my last friends.

By the time I sold my house, rodents had chewed the pipes five times. The universe hated me. I could never catch a break. Bitter and angry again.

My Perfect Storm

Ashcroft

I started looking out of town and ended up buying a house and moving to Ashcroft, B.C., a little village in the middle of nowhere. The house I bought was amazing, and the view of the mountains from my deck and living room was great. As I was moving in, my neighbours came by and introduced themselves. Living in a small village was neat. I felt welcomed by my neighbours.

Starting anew in Ashcroft, B.C.

Because I worked three hours away in Vancouver, I drove back and forth each week. I sold my little Dodge truck and bought myself a big-ass truck and camper so I could sleep in the camper while I was in Vancouver for the week of work.

Comfort from the Storm?

Learning how to laugh again

Life was pretty good. I was still lonely, though. I was doing shrooms once a month and felt better than ever. I went to Vancouver Island once and did them with friends. On our 'trip,' we laughed so hard all night. It was great. I was learning how to laugh again. My freedom was coming back. I was starting to think I could make it through. The cloud over me was disappearing.

I was also finding that if I did a THC gummy bear, it would help relieve tension, as I had so much physical stress from over the years of torture on my body, from the accident early on to biking accidents and many other injuries.

The camper I bought to sleep in at work was also a nightmare. It had a lot of problems, and again, it seemed like I never got a break.

It was summer again, and I looked forward to riding my Harley back and forth to work.

An eye-opening trip

Sometimes, I wouldn't do any mushrooms for quite a while. There was one mushroom trip where I experienced forgiveness for myself and others. It was bizarre.

I had a major awareness during that trip. It dawned on me that I went to friends for help, and they wouldn't help me. I would get angry, then go to different people, and so on and so forth and then go back to the same people. This continued for years, but I realized this wasn't true. It's not that they wouldn't help; it was that they couldn't help me.

What a concept! A feeling of freedom swept over me. Resentments shed and, once again, more room for new things to flow through me.

Taking notice

The next day, I was going to the Soberider AGM, and there were a lot of people there I had grudges with, but I felt different this time. I had a shift. I knew I just needed to look at the stories differently. It was like shedding 200 pounds.

People noticed changes. They said it was like I was lighter, and the darkness was leaving. People who did notice and asked what I did, I said magic mushrooms. I believe if I have to keep it a secret, then it's not healthy for me. So, it was out, and I was less judged as others were noticing a change in my anger. Today, I know there are people I'm getting close with who stayed away from me because I was too toxic. And I was.

Head-on

A few days after the AGM, I was leaving work at lunch and got into a head-on collision with a car. According to the damage done to the car, I shouldn't have walked away from it.

I was riding at least 40-60 km/hr, and the car was doing at least that, but I walked away from it. I took Friday off and, of course, the weekend, then back to work on Monday.

Friday, on the way home, I stopped and bought a used 2003 Harley Dyna to ride so I wouldn't have to spend the summer without a bike, as I thought this was some of my therapy.

Comfort from the Storm?

I did magic mushrooms that weekend when I was in a negative mood, and what a trip. I got sick to start, then I started to panic and thought life was over, spurred on by the accident. I hid in my room under the covers and panicked. I have never felt panic like this before.

Then the phone rang. It was Mike. I didn't want to answer it because he was clean, and I didn't want him to say I told you so. However, I answered, and that was not what I got. He supported me, we laughed, and he listened to the craziness of my trip.

I learned a big lesson that night. I learned that mushrooms really enhance what you're feeling when you take them. A lesson learned for the next time, for sure. However, I think from this experience, I stretched my boundaries and comfort zone.

By this time, I was becoming more aware that most people weren't like me. I was trying things that typical people in 12-step rooms, who I've come to know over the years, DO NOT do. However, I didn't hide what I was doing. I felt that if you had to hide it, it must be wrong.

I was having some shifts in my life with taking mushrooms and gummy bears, but now I had some new fear arising. In a week, I was about to take a personal development course that I signed up for. What new challenge would that bring?

Butt-fuck Alberta

At this point, work was going better than ever. I fit in, life was good, and I didn't want to go on this course.

Not only did I not want to screw up what seemed pretty good at the time, but the course was also in butt-fuck Alberta.

My Perfect Storm

I decided to head out early for this course and stopped in to see my friends, Mike and Nancy, on the way before driving to Medicine Hat, Alberta. It was only five hours from Mike's.

Covid was still rampant, but some restrictions were lifted. Many places wouldn't let you into their business due to restrictions, and for me, it was like the government saying, "Fuck you." I felt like this whole Covid thing was a bunch of sick lies and bullshit from the government.

Anyhow, by the time I got there, I was angry. I didn't even want to be there. I would have had a better time riding my bike even though I was still sore from the accident the week before.

Angry and antisocial, I drove up to the ranch where the course was being held for a week. The first thing we did was to choose the room we were going to sleep in, and of course, I had to share it with someone. I actually brought my coffee maker with me because you know I need a good coffee.

Our first meeting and time to share started off rough. I was challenged right from that point on. The course ended up being extremely transformational for me.

I was challenged every day in this course, and to this day, I guess I was just ready for it. I showed up and participated even when I thought that sometimes, the stuff we were doing was pretty stupid. I cried a lot. I connected with people, and we picked buddies, and mine was Doug. He was from Vancouver. I was different from Doug, but I think we did connect and still keep in contact to this day.

There was a reflective time when we had to write our hopes, dreams, and goals for our future. I struggled with this exercise. I wrote some limp dick hopes and dreams and then went to sleep.

Comfort from the Storm?

I woke up in the early morning lying in bed, and BAM, the thought—*you fucken' ripped yourself off again. Get your ass out of bed and write some dreams on that paper*—ran through my head.

I got out of bed and wrote: I want a woman in my life, a partner, a lover. I want someone to love and grow with. I was excited.

So, we did high ropes exercises, and Philippe was there. He was a volunteer. He asked me about my goal. I said I wanted a relationship in my life. He gave me some of the best advice I have ever been given, and I still use it to this day.

I had to sit out on one event due to the physical nature that was required since I was just in a head-on collision about two weeks before. This hurt my ego even though I chose to bench myself for the betterment of the team's success. I participated in the activity from the sidelines, along with a few other members who opted out, too. I gave my all that week and was rewarded with growth.

After the exercise, one of the guys there was having a meltdown. I hugged him, and next thing you know, everyone was in a big team hug. For some reason, I felt like Tuomas needed to be rocked, so I started to rock him. There were more than 30 people in this hug. My first thought was *I would never do this*, but I continued. I got the whole group rocking. It was a moment of see what you can do when you decide.

One exercise we did was a blindfold obstacle course. My friend Lance was having a hard time. We were in silent mode, so no talking. He had spoken and confessed, "I quit." I encouraged him to stay. I was attempting to give him my positive energy.

The experience I had with helping Lance was noted by one of the coaches; however, not in the way I thought about it. Tim, the coach, said to me, "You give yourself freely and then get resentful." I went to bite back and say something, but it occurred to me that I did live my life full of resentment. He was right.

Tim, the coach, took me aside at the end and told me I was in the top three people for being leaders in our group. I'm proud of this, as it means I made a difference.

CHAPTER 15

Life with Sunnier Days

My real growth

I believe this was when my real growth started, or at least it's when I started to understand that I could turn things around. I also gained some new friends who would go to the wall for me. So, on the second-to-last day of the course, I felt alive and free. For once, I wasn't bottled up with anger and resentment. However, I had been here before, and I had stopped doing the work.

My Perfect Storm

Today, I know I'm responsible for my life, and what I put in is what I get out. It's like food for my diabetes. Eat healthy, and my count stays down. The same works for the flow of me. If I keep positivity flowing, it helps to clean out the garbage. Today, I am responsible.

I met lots of people throughout the week. One woman that I met during the week was Lisa. I was having meals with her, getting to know her a little more. I liked her and gave her the respect both of us deserved to focus on ourselves that week.

Lisa and I were talking, and we both thought the course went until Sunday; however, it ended on Saturday. Then what came out of my mouth was, "I guess we're going for dinner tonight, then?"

She said, "Yes," and the rest is history, as they say. We have been together since.

Even though we hadn't even talked very much during the week or thought about being together, we ended up going from the ranch to a hotel room. Lisa gave me so much that day. Her kindness and gentleness are things I've never experienced before in my life.

I had the next week off work, so after our goodbyes, I drove home, got my bike, and went back to Calgary to see Lisa.

Tim, one of the facilitators from the week at the ranch, was putting on a free workshop about relationships. It was only three hours, and it was one of the best three-hour dates I've had with Lisa.

I learned how I could be more effective in our relationship. Tim had challenged my beliefs of what I thought I knew about being a partner and a lover and how selfish I was in relationships.

Besides meeting Lisa, work was going great. I was feeling the best I had ever felt.

Being that Lisa and I were in two different provinces, we were flying back and forth to see each other. The government started talking like they were going to make the jab for Covid mandatory for flying, so I broke down and got mine just for my own peace of mind. I knew that if I went to the airport and they said I couldn't go see Lisa, I would have lost my shit, so I knew, for that reason only, I had to get the shot.

I had challenged Lisa to get certified to be able to scuba dive with me. She rose to the challenge and took the classes.

More BS

Working in the movie Industry was becoming less and less enjoyable. They started to play games, so I played back. There was BS around my job and the duties that were expected. I was stuck between two unions, and it escalated from there.

Mexico

For the Christmas holidays, Lisa and I made plans to go to Mexico. I drove to Lisa's house from Vancouver. It was a long drive through the mountains during the winter conditions, but it was way worth it.

Lisa's daughter, Brianna, and I were talking a little bit more and getting to know each other. Jordan came over for Christmas dinner, and it was great to get to know him a little bit more, too.

My Perfect Storm

Lisa and I drove up to Red Deer a few times to see Mike and Nancy. It was fun.

By late December, Lisa and I were off to Mexico on our first holiday together. It was great but different for both of us. I was used to being alone and travelling alone. Lisa was used to being married (previously for 26 years) and travelling with kids. We had a great time getting to know each other more.

Lisa passed her certification in Mexico, so it was time to dive together. We made plans to go diving the next day. However, Lisa woke up not feeling well and thought she might have Covid. Turns out, it was Covid.

When we tested for Covid before flying home, my result was negative, and Lisa's was positive. So now came the stress of rescheduling flights and getting back home. It was such a busy time of year (with all the Covid crap) that airlines didn't answer their phones. We drove out to the airport on the day we were originally meant to fly out. Lisa said earlier that day that whoever could fly home must go home first.

The airlines informed me that since my test result said I didn't have Covid, I could fly home. I had to rush as the gates were about to close. At that point, I knew I was leaving Lisa there. I still remember the look on her face, knowing that I was leaving her there. To me, she looked scared. She insisted I go, but I felt like an asshole. I was sure we would be done. Lisa kept insisting she was ok.

We talked on Zoom a few times a day, and I watched her soar. This was her first time managing such a unique experience in Mexico by herself. I saw her gain confidence in herself, and it was one of the coolest things I have witnessed.

When I returned to Calgary, I drove back to Vancouver to work. My truck's def fluid had frozen; what a nightmare. More stupid shit from the government for this green bullshit.

I tested positive for Covid at work, so I had two weeks off, paid. My truck needed to go to the shop, so I rented a car and drove back to Ashcroft. They called the next day and said it was fixed.

I booked a flight to Calgary, drove back to Vancouver, and flew to Calgary. Yes, as you can tell, I think all the crap around Covid is bullshit, and I don't believe it. I'm not a very politically correct person, and the only thing I'll say is it's rare that the government tells us the truth.

I kept pushing off going back to work and did my best to drag out the time I needed to take off for Covid. I was just starting to unwind from all the bullshit and games, questioning why this shit always happened to me.

90-day goal-setting course

I was still seeing Kimberly once a week on Zoom. The next big coaching course was starting soon; it was based out of Calgary. It was a 90-day goal-setting course that was mostly online, but there were some in-person events, too.

I decided to stay in Calgary and stretch out my time away from work and work on myself. There was too much drama and bullying there for me. I seemed to get fucked over all the time. I know I get easily triggered, and I don't know how to respond.

Red flags

The first weekend of the course came, and there were red flags everywhere for me. Some people needed to take over control of just naming our group, and goal setting was not the emphasis at all. The real focus was to enroll other people in this personal development work. I lost my cool and was ready to quit from the get-go. I felt like I got suckered into paying for a goal-setting course when it wasn't that at all. This was not what I paid for.

The personal development courses were put on by the Personal Success Institute. This 90-day course was called PLD (Pacesetter Leadership Dynamics).

During this first weekend, I felt again like I wasn't being heard. I had a conflict with the times I needed to attend the course and be at work. A bunch of shit came up for me because of this conflict.

I approached the lead coordinator, Joelle, about finding a solution to the overlap of my work schedule and the online meetings. Joelle put her hand in my face and said I want solutions, not problems and walked away. Then, the next day, Joelle had the audacity to call me the bully, which was a trigger for me, so I believed her. When we met in person on the opening weekend, Joelle said, "I will do or say whatever I need to say to get what I want you to say or do."

Over the course, I felt like she was the bully. From this rude initial confrontation to the way she treated others on Zoom calls, it all rubbed me the wrong way. All I was trying to figure out was how I would do this insane course with my work.

This course reminded me that I don't like being lied to. During the whole course, I felt like it was all based on a lie. If they had said from the get-go that it was an enrollment course, then I would have gotten my money back and quit.

It was three months long, and having this initial feeling of disgust was gruelling for me.

My goal

My goal was to become a coach and live a more meaningful life.

For this course, I had coach calls every morning, but they weren't there to help me fulfill my goal of becoming a coach; they had their own agenda. Every day, all I heard was: give me numbers of how many people you'll enroll in this work.

I really began to lose my trust in the PSI style of business. I think I wanted to quit five or more times a week.

For me, there was a true lack of respect from the business. The PSI office was disorganized and continually fell short.

I fought with it. I gave them back what they gave others. They didn't like it, but I didn't back down.

My recurring theme

This has been a recurring theme in my life. I was experiencing the bullshit again, and life was screaming at me. I didn't fit in anywhere. If it wasn't for Lisa putting up with me and weekly Zoom meetings with Kimberly, my therapist, I would've quit.

My Perfect Storm

I fought with the area director lots and even had a Zoom call with the corporate office. I was promised the friends I signed up to take this three-day course would be looked after, and this didn't happen. This really sucked because it undermined my once great faith in PSI and my own integrity.

With the agenda of pushing enrollment, I ended up pushing away my good friend Mike and his wife, Nancy. They thought my assertiveness on the push to enroll was too much, and they wanted me out of their lives.

On one of the weekends, we needed to pick big goals, and, somehow, mine was that Lisa and I go to Thailand this year. We had 24 hours to complete the goal, so I booked the tickets for us to go. At least, this was one good thing that happened in the course.

I believe in personal development, but the way I saw the PSI office treat people was very poor, and I've experienced the same treatment firsthand.

I would fight with the coach that I was assigned to because, for me, it was all a big lie. I stayed because I paid for it, and I know I am not a quitter. Kimberly kept telling me, "One day, you'll be able to use this experience in your own coaching business."

I was screaming for help to get past my lack of trust, and all they would do was shove their agenda at me. They had the audacity to say, "What are you screaming about?" after repeated requests to be heard and supported. I felt that there was no care for my well-being, and I felt that they didn't care and were just happy to have my money.

I felt so bitter about this course and was happy to get a break, so I attended a men's leadership seminar that I had already paid for. The men's leadership seminar was a good course, although I don't feel like

I was fully present as my head was so spun from the PLD course and the disgust I was feeling about PSI.

I was so frustrated that they had one of the corporate people call to offer to buy me out of the course. I told her I needed time to think about it. I called a few people who had quit previously to get some advice from them. There were 11 days left, so I decided to stick it out.

The last weekend

The last weekend of PLD was a whole weekend away at a retreat, and I made sure to attend so I could get my last two cents in about how this course treated me. I didn't participate very much; I was just there.

This weekend was filled with more of their bullshit. They had an acknowledgment ceremony where participants were acknowledged when they enrolled six people into the basic personal development class.

Well, I was actually very good at enrolling, and I made this quota. I confirmed my achievement, but they didn't recognize me like the rest. They said that these six weren't confirmed, even though it was easy to name off the exact names of those who signed up under me.

Lisa was so supportive throughout the entire event. I couldn't ask for a better lover, partner, or friend.

About six months later, I realized how much I had learned from that 90-day goal-setting course despite the bull shit. I had grown and gained a voice, and most of the time, I realized that I could remain calmer when presented with turmoil. Today, I still have trouble with people hearing what I say. So, I'm glad I didn't quit. I look back and feel like I won. I have more calmness.

My Perfect Storm

Not working

I had a lot of time on my hands not working. So, I took it upon myself to cook, clean, and do the shopping for the house in Calgary, where I was staying with Lisa. I was working through the online coaching course so I could become a coach myself and found the tech part hard. I was just starting to dive deep into the land of computer work. All the computer stress from the PLD game was really taking a toll on my self-esteem. My buttons were being pushed to the max. I felt stupid.

I was finding out just how illiterate I was and how hard computers are to navigate. This was one of the things I always thought I was ok with, but being almost illiterate brings me great pain when I'm faced with new challenges.

I chose to make breakfast for Lisa every morning before she headed off for work. This I knew I was good at. It was interesting, though; it seemed that Lisa was having a hard time letting me look after her. When we talked about it, we were able to see that this is what she was used to in her previous marriage. She always just 'did it' and didn't expect someone else to step up and do this for her. It was great talking to her about this. I think she sees now that I enjoy and love looking after her.

Remember that great advice from Phillipe I mentioned earlier? Well, in the morning, we ask each other how we can love each other that day, and when we go to bed, we ask if we have fulfilled our commitment for the day. I was learning how to love someone the way they wanted to be loved.

I love watching our relationship grow. I finally met someone who loves me for me. We are great together; we support and cherish each other. She was a rock for me with all the other stress that was going on in my life. Learning to talk and share what was going on for us was the key.

Life with Sunnier Days

Part of this PSI and PLD course was to gain a community of supporters, but I still struggled a lot when no one called me. People just gave excuses like, "Nobody calls anymore," but I knew that I needed phone calls because texts never really kept me connected with people. It still feels like no one cares. My buddies, Mike and Mark, are about the only two in my life who seem to care. Oh, and Lisa, of course.

Summer!

I was getting excited as summer was coming, and my bike was almost fixed from the accident. I finally got both my Harleys to Calgary. My green Dyna and my newly painted Road Glide.

Scott's newly painted and rebuilt Road Glide.

Tara, my niece, flew in from Toronto, and Mike came to take the basic three-day personal development course, riding his bike out from Kamloops. Later, of course, we all got to go riding. I was so proud of Tara. It's nice having at least one close family member in my life.

Toronto

Carrie-Anne, a girl I had met in PLD, called and asked if I would help her staff the three-day course in Toronto. I said yes. I went a few days before and stayed a few days after. I saw Uncle Joe, Aunt Sandra, and Phyllis. I went to an A.A. meeting and saw Martin, who was my first sponsor in the A.A. program. It was a great trip. The guilty feeling or just the sad feeling of not seeing my brothers, sister, and mom wasn't there anymore. I have healed a lot.

Staffing those three days was one of the best experiences of my life. I felt compassion much deeper than ever watching people work their way through personal challenges during the course. I cried a lot as well. I felt a connection and purpose. After staffing, I saw how much we benefit from the work, so I got inspired again.

Marry in 30 days!

As part of the course, staff volunteers must pick a 30-day goal. Lisa and I had talked about getting married, so I picked a goal that Lisa and I would marry in 30 days.

I called Lisa and told her that my 30-day goal was to marry her. I asked her if she liked the goal. She, of course, said yes and was ecstatic to marry me. *Silly girl.*

Life with Sunnier Days

We were married on July 23, 2022, in our small backyard in Calgary. It was a great day! Brianna and Jordan were part of our wedding day and welcomed me into the family. Mike, Mark, and Lorie were there, too. My buddy Doug from Vancouver also drove in for our wedding. It was so great that they were part of our day.

The day we got married, Lisa was so stressed out. I told her that we needed to get out and go for a ride first. She kind of freaked out about the idea, but I think she trusted me and my ideas, so I informed everyone that we were going riding. We rode out to Bragg Creek for coffee and a snack. It helped Lisa relax. I'm glad I suggested it.

Cross Canada trip

A few days after our wedding, on June 25th, I got on my Harley and started the trip to Prince Edward Island to meet Lisa's family. It rained a lot, and it was cold riding across the prairies. About halfway through the trip, I dropped my cell phone on the Trans-Canada Highway while texting and riding and broke it. I contacted Lisa (via Wi-Fi on my iPad), and she made an appointment at Apple in Winnipeg, Manitoba, where I got myself a new phone.

I stopped in Kenora, Ontario, to see my cousin Kellie. It was great to see her since it had been a few years.

Being that it was cold and raining most of the trip, it wasn't as fun as it could've been. I reached P.E.I one day before Lisa arrived.

I stayed at Lisa's dad's house. At this point, I hadn't met Peter in person. Peter wanted me to stay at his house when I arrived, and he had told Lisa that he would insist I take his bedroom as it was the only one in the house.

My Perfect Storm

I told Lisa I wouldn't think about taking the bed of a 78-year-old man. Peter and I had some words about it. I insisted on sleeping on the floor. It was a little tense, but he finally heard me, and I slept that night on the floor.

P.E.I.

Lisa arrived by plane the next day, and we had a great time in P.E.I. We spent a lot of time exploring and having fun with the family and meeting up with some of her friends. You see, Lisa grew up there, and I had never been before.

We had two great lobster feasts two nights in a row. I also had a lot of fun teasing Lisa's niece and nephew, Jack and Aimee.

We were there for two weeks, then Lisa and I rode back to Calgary together on the Harley. It was a great trip. We rode to Hamilton in two days and saw Phyllis and an old buddy, Warren. We hung out with my Uncle Joe and Aunt Sandra. Looking back, I really appreciated hanging out and catching up. You see, this was the last time I saw my Uncle Joe.

During our time in Ontario, we rode out to Port Dover to see where bikers go on an annual ride every Friday the 13th. I hadn't been there since I was a kid. The popularity of this annual event is great for local store owners.

It was a great trip down memory lane, meeting up with family and friends. I loved that I got to share Niagara Falls with Lisa, too.

We also rode across the states. Lisa did great on the back of the bike. We did some really long days that I know Lisa hadn't done before on a motorcycle.

Life with Sunnier Days

I was a little bummed out that we had to rush the trip to get back home. We had to get back to pack up Lisa's Calgary house so it could to be rented out. After the Calgary house was cleaned out, we took all the stuff up to our house in Ashcroft with help from our friends Mike and Mark.

We had a little downtime in Ashcroft before we were on our way to another PSI personal development course in Albuquerque, New Mexico. It was a big yearly event.

Albuquerque

In Albuquerque, we had fun and met lots of great people, but not many of them stayed in touch after the event. I see this has happened a lot in my life, and I have come to be ok with it.

During one of the exercises, we did some goal-setting. First, we started 10 years out and worked our way back. Somehow, having my brother Ted back in my life got put on the list. This scared me and was kind of fucked-up. Why did I want him back in my life when all we ever did was screw each other around?

I also had this huge meltdown. I was terrified to move forward, not feeling like I was worthy or I deserved it.

While in Albuquerque, they announced a new course they were putting on. It was expensive, but I wanted to go. It sounded like a course that would help me with my coaching business. I talked to Lisa, and she said, "Of course, you should sign up."

The next day, Lisa asked me, "Why don't I sign up, too?"

My Perfect Storm

Lisa ended up signing up after having a chat with Tim, one of the facilitators.

We only had a week when we arrived back from Albuquerque before our big trip to Thailand.

CHAPTER 16

More Calm and Radiance

Thailand

We landed in Thailand on September 29th with no booked tickets to return. Lisa and I spent a few days in Bangkok and went to the 50-foot Buddha. It was very cool. Bangkok was a little too busy for my liking; it's a place we would never decide to live in.

In Bangkok, we caught a cab to Hua Hin. My friend from Canada, John, was living there with his wife, Tiki.

My Perfect Storm

John had suggested we stay at the one-bedroom condo they had previously rented. It was a great spot.

We rented a scooter and started to explore the night markets. They were fun. The Thai people were so friendly. We loved going for dinners. The food was amazing.

However, my diabetes counts were high, so I had to buckle down and pay close attention to what I ate; I did find it was easier here in Thailand than in Canada to monitor my diabetes with food.

What a cultural difference compared to Canada. We saw a family of four or more cramped on a scooter. Kids holding on, too, and very few were wearing helmets. It reminded me of what it was like when I was a kid, like riding on the top of a load in the back of a pick-up truck.

I also saw workers on the back of a truck (not strapped on or with a harness on), just holding the water hose to water plants as the water truck drove down the road. Thailand seemed carefree with fewer restrictions. I was loving it. I think this way of life breeds more confidence.

We planned our first trip to the Island of Koh Tao so we could go diving. Lisa booked this great room overlooking the ocean. It was beautiful, and the diving was good. We dove for our first time together here.

Cancer is back

When we were in Koh Tao, I had a phone call with my medical specialist and found out my P.S.A. (Prostate-Specific Antigen) level was detectable again. I was devastated. This meant my cancer was back.

More Calm and Radiance

Lisa had to take a refresher course to go out diving, so I went out exploring with the scooter, and I felt angry, wanting to fight or give up when it then dawned on me that I didn't have to fight. I just had to show up and take direction or not. I've learned I've had to fight everything in my life, so I decided I wasn't fighting.

We decided to take public transit back to Hua Hin. We boarded a 5 ½ hour bus ride back from Koh Tao after the ferry ride to the mainland.

Back in Hua Hin, I was getting excited as Brianna and Jordan were coming to Thailand for Christmas. I was looking forward to getting to know Jordan a bit better. We had not spent much time together so far.

We spent our time riding around and going for dinners with Tiki and John. John introduced us to their friend, Terry and his wife, Nam. We also met Bob and Nok. They are all great people.

At this point, we had been in Thailand for about three months, so we made our way to immigration to see about doing a border run and resetting our visas. Just before the kids came, we booked tickets to Vietnam as a destination to reset our visas.

The trip to Vietnam wasn't that good for me. It was cold, raining, the food sucked, and I was having a hard time with my diabetes. I felt that the Vietnamese people were quite rude as well. However, it dawned on me while we were taking a rest on one of our excursions that what I was feeling from the people was what I was putting out there. So, I decided to change my attitude and approach people with a positive attitude. The trip went better, but it was hard to keep my diabetes under control.

Going to Marble Mountain was the highlight of this trip. The craftsmanship in the carvings was amazing. I love getting out and seeing the beauty. It helped shift my attitude as well.

My Perfect Storm

In the last few days in Vietnam, Lisa was excited to hear that the kids were at the Calgary airport about to board to Vancouver, then Tokyo, and then we would meet them in Bangkok. They updated us that they missed their plane in Vancouver and the only flight out to Thailand would be five days later.

Brianna and Jordan couldn't do that, so after three days in Vancouver, they flew back home to Calgary. We were very disappointed and upset that they wouldn't be celebrating Christmas with us in Thailand. They ended up having to rebook to come see us in February.

Mushroom source

I had been looking for a mushroom source as I felt ready to do more. I hadn't done them since I met Lisa, but I found a source. I did my first 'trip' in Thailand with a friend, and it was great. I started to go into the journey, and the demons were coming. This was intensely uncomfortable, so I said to myself, *I am in charge of this journey*. After making this shift, my journey was full of love and gratitude. It was my first 'trip' like this.

The big coaching course was starting soon. I was stoked and was looking forward to it. Lisa and I began in the same group, and I was looking forward to working with her. The sessions started, and we had our first week together. The second week, I showed up, and our coach said to me, "Scott, what are you doing here? You're being taken out of this group because family members shouldn't be in the same class."

It took until the end of week three to figure out who my new group was and when my new meeting time was. At this point, I was missing out. Missing out on getting to know my new group. Missing out on an expensive course I paid a lot of money for. Seemed like the running story in my life. It also felt like the same disorganization from PSI.

More Calm and Radiance

I did my best to roll with it, and I thought they would have just kept it simple, but all I saw was that corporate office bullshit operating the same way I saw Calgary being run. A brutal lack of communication skills was affecting me and my success again.

I found myself angry and frustrated with the PSI office again. They sold me on a concept, and they were not delivering once again. It was so frustrating to go back and forth with emails, trying to solve times of meetings and so on. Their lack of communication skills or care was a recurring event for me with PSI.

This time, I quit and got them to give me my money back. I knew that the mental strain and toll that the last PLD course had on me wasn't good, so I decided that removing myself early from the course was the best choice for me. This was one of the first times I took responsibility and quit something. I felt like I did everything I could before I made the decision.

My brother Ted

A goal I had made when I was in the course back in Albuquerque was to have my brother Ted back in my life. Well, after almost 30 years of not connecting, we were talking on video calls for an hour at a time. I just found out that Ted's wife left him. I was thankful to be there for him. We started to get to know each other. It's been different. I have had to change a lot of stories that I've told myself for years regarding Ted and our relationship.

The last part of our trip was spent in Koh Chang. I'm thankful for the audiobooks I was introduced to. One story that I will always recommend is *The Untethered Soul* by Michael Singer.

My Perfect Storm

Another trip

I decided to do another mushroom journey. This particular mushroom trip was painful and full of regret and sorrow for the way my family turned out. Also, the mistrust and huge lack of integrity with the personal development company I've taken courses from was weighing heavy on me.

As painful as the journey was, it was very healing looking at the things I have held onto. At the beginning of the journey, I felt my dad looking down at my family with sorrow and regret for how we had turned out.

As I talked more with Ted, it was clear that our mother had pitted us against each other. The journey I have gone on has helped me process my life. I don't get it, but I know it works.

I was shaken, and my head hurt for a few days after this journey. Then, I realized that I was able to grieve for myself and my family for the first time. The anger I've always felt was gone.

We had to reset our Thai visas again, so we decided to go to Cambodia. This was a trip of a lifetime.

We went to Siem Reap and saw Angkor Wat. It was three days of temples. They were amazing to see. Being a stonemason, I marvelled at the craftsmanship.

Then we went to Phnom Penh to see the Killing Fields. I was horrified at how people were treated during the Khmer Rouge Regime. I learned that over two million people were killed (which was even more than Hitler killed). I got quite emotional there. Why do we people treat other people like this? I believe we're still doing this. It just looks a little different.

More Calm and Radiance

For me, it was a new awareness. I felt like I was thawing, discovering that I really do have more compassion within me. I love growing and changing into the man I would like to be.

The last part of our Thailand trip was spent in Koh Chang. I got to do some more diving and hang out with my friend, Cliff. It was fun. I also got a new tattoo that I had wanted for years, one dedicated to the many people (and pets) that have been in my life. The idea for what the tattoo would look like came to me after diving one day. The tattoo was a memorial for Sherie, the girl whose death really affected me many years ago. I also added people that have contributed to my life.

This is Scott's latest tattoo in memory of those who died and had an effect on him.

My Perfect Storm

The trip back to Canada was long, and the jet lag was gross. The second week on Canadian soil was a little bitter for me.

Within a week of returning to Canada, Lisa was staffing that three-day course like I did back in Toronto. I originally was going to staff with Lisa; however, I decided I needed to pull away from PSI and didn't end up staffing with her in Vancouver.

I've had a hard time dealing with the cost of living in Canada and the cost of stuff like groceries. My mood was a bit all over the place. Angry that our own government treats their own people like this.

My Dart

I was scheduled to pick up my newly-restored 1969 Dodge Dart and, again, was confronted with people who didn't have integrity in their service or the way they dealt with me.

Before driving 10 hours with Lisa to go get the car, I was told it would be completed, and I could pick it up. I totally lost my shit when I got there, and they informed me it wasn't done yet. There was no courtesy phone call to say, "I think we may need more time."

I really have a hard time with people being wishy-washy around me. I just need a clear answer. I can deal with a clear answer. The way this situation played out reminded me that other people often don't take ownership, and this is so hard for me to deal with.

So, after leaving my car there, I flew back two weeks later to pick it up. When I arrived, I was greatly disappointed that the bodywork was shoddy and that, for me, dealing with people is often a nightmare.

More Calm and Radiance

I decided to take the car back home for the 11-hour drive with the poorly completed bodywork. I was so pissed. It took weeks to finally get that ironed out and to have the company step up and fix their work. It was a real pain.

Scott's childhood dream car – 1969 Dodge Dart.

May 22, 2023, was a big day. I was in our Ashcroft home with Lisa. My life was great, and I was 20 years clean and sober.

My Perfect Storm

I still struggle to see or experience joy. I have fleeting glimpses of this. Most people would celebrate reaching such a milestone in their lives, but I struggle with having feelings of excitement over such things. I know Lisa and my close friends Mike and Mark were more excited about my 20 years of sobriety than I was. I'm so hard on myself, but this is slowly getting better.

The rock Lisa gave Scott to signify his 20 years of sobriety.

Service for my brother and niece

A memorial service was being held for my older brother, Gary, and his deceased daughter, Glennis, an hour away from where I lived in Kamloops. They both passed away several years prior, but the planned service was a simple ceremony that some of my family members were planning to attend.

More Calm and Radiance

My aunt Cathy was coming up from the U.S., and my brother Ted and his daughter Barbara Jo were flying in from Ontario. I found out that my mother was accompanying them as well.

When I was talking to Aunt Cathy, my mom's sister, she asked me if I was going to behave with my mom when she came to visit. I thought for a bit and replied, "It's not me who needs to behave; it's my mom who needs that reminder."

After that, I believe Aunt Cathy ended up asking her not to stir crap up.

I talked with Ted about picking him, B.J., and mom up at the airport. After our conversation, it was nice to hear that Ted and I were on the same team, or at least he was hearing what my concerns were with mom. I sometimes wonder what it would be like for my mom to know she pushes people away and that her kids don't like her; we just tolerate her. She raised kids who don't talk to each other too.

Picking up Ted, Barbra Jo, and my mom at the airport went fairly smoothly. The ride back to my house was rather uneventful but awkward as I was always on guard, wondering when mom was going to crack and act out.

We stopped at Hell's Gate. No, really, no pun intended, that's what it's called. It's this large, suspended gondola over the treacherous Fraser River. I had been there before, but Barbara Jo had never been through the mountains, so it was great to be part of her first time seeing such an amazing site.

It was nice that I was able to not let my stuff with my mom interfere with having a great day. We went back to our house, and Mark cooked us dinner. It was great and uneventful. I was a little in shock that my mother had gone all day without stirring things up. Also, I had

My Perfect Storm

to bite my tongue at times to not stir the pot, something that takes effort for me at times.

Ted and I were getting along fairly well. We had some decent conversations, even with our rough connection growing up. Who would have ever thought this was possible? Not me.

So onward to the next stress of going to the memorial service. My niece, Mary, and Gloria, my sister-in-law, organized the memorial service. I hadn't seen them in eight years. I hadn't been welcomed there for such a long time. Mary had stopped talking to me at her dad's funeral many years ago because I had a strained interaction with my mother and left instead of causing a scene and losing my cool.

I spent the whole time during the service a little on guard, waiting for my mom to act out. Things went well. It was a little nerve-wracking not knowing how to be around people who had a sketchy past with me. However, with the help of Ted and Aunt Cathy, it went smoothly.

I was struggling with the memorial service idea. It made me think that people seem to care more for people when they die rather than put more energy into their relationships when they're alive.

My mom stayed with Cathy, so I didn't have to spend too much time with her. Ted and Barbara Jo stayed at our house for the last two nights before going home.

Ted, BJ, Lisa, and I drove to Whistler. It was great seeing BJ's face light up when she saw the mountains. It was great to have family time.

I was sad when they left and drove them back to the airport. I had a good time with my brother and niece. It was a great start.

More Calm and Radiance

I did talk with Ted a little about the fact that it's time for our family to start healing. I saw how far the denial and need to be right were so strong in our family and how much pain this caused.

It was ingrained into us that each of us wasn't worthy and had to fight to get anything and anywhere. It takes a lot of work and energy to change.

Cross Canada trip

By mid-June, Lisa and I were busy getting ready for our trek across Canada for Lisa to launch her first book, *A Year of Love*, which became an Amazon best seller.

The drive east was great. Lisa and I connected and talked a lot. We listened to many audiobooks, from *The Six Pillars Of Self-Esteem* to *The Untethered Soul*. We worked on editing this book you're reading right now, and on this trip, we figured out the title, which went from *Creating a King* to *My Perfect Storm*. We loved camping in our little trailer, and we sold some of Lisa's books along the way, too.

On the drive down, we booked a campsite at Kill Bear Park for our return drive home. You see, the first traumatic experience of my life happened here, and I decided that I needed to revisit this place since I was in a much better place in my life. I wanted to have a happier, more joyful experience here. This is where I decided to end my book.

As we travelled across Canada, we stopped in Ontario to attend a family wedding. Morgan, my niece's daughter, was getting married. I had never met Morgan.

I was a little stressed. A long time ago, I partied a lot with some of the people who were attending the wedding, and I caused a lot of damage.

My Perfect Storm

Dave was there, and after all these years, I felt bad about what I did to him and feared a rebuttal. However, there was none. Dave kept his distance from me and I from him. Later, I learned that Dave was angry for a long time as he questioned whether his younger son was really his. Dave assumed for many years that his son, Mike, could have been my child. The damage we do that we don't even know about.

I knew there would be drinking at the wedding, which opens a door for anything to happen. However, the wedding was great, and I felt welcomed as if nothing ever happened in our past.

CHAPTER 17

Embracing the Warmth of the Sun, the Wind in My Hair, and the Blue Skies

Connecting

We spent the next week at Ted's, getting to know him and his wife, Ty. It was hard seeing my family in pain and denial, not willing to look at themselves. I spent years staying away because I needed to focus on myself and getting healthier.

My Perfect Storm

Ty told me she was scared to meet me. We actually had great conversations and I did ask her if she really heard all sides of that story.

Looking at life from the place I was to where I am now helps me look at things differently. It makes me sad to see many people just keep doing the daily grind of life. Doing the same thing over and over, thinking things will be different. Having to cling to thinking they're right even when someone else is hurting. We cling to the fact that we have a nice house, good job, and money to live, thinking we've made it. Often, we are too scared to let go and just love people.

I wish things could be different for more people. Although, I know life is about baby steps. I know today I have a voice, and I can be heard. Today, I am making a difference in people's lives.

It took a lot of time and effort to change my own life. I see how the environment and people I was surrounded by were the recipe for my perfect storm.

It was during a conversation with Ty that helped tweak the title, *My Perfect Storm*. That was a great suggestion. Thanks, Ty.

Lisa and I travelled by the seat of our pants, with no defined plans, only a final destination of P.E.I.

We saw Phyllis (aka mom) a few more times. They were great visits. I'm grateful to have time with her as I know her time on this Earth is getting shorter, and she has been so influential in my life, always believing in me.

Embracing the Warmth of the Sun, the Wind in My Hair, and the Blue Skies

Phyllis (mom) and Scott

I'm happy about one thing. I'm getting a voice. Spending time with Phyllis helped show me how much I've changed. We talked about our beliefs, as mine have changed from the man who thought he had to go to A.A. for the rest of his life to the man who knows it's all about the choices and decisions I make.

It was also great to meet Phyllis's care aid, Leeza. I got to see how great this lady is and how she takes care of my mom. Lisa and Leeza did some meal prep for Phyllis. We had a great time together.

I felt a great sense of sadness when we left. I hope I see Phyllis for a few more years.

We packed up once again and drove to Ottawa to see Lisa's brother, Dean, his wife, Yvonne, and their kids, Gavin and Carter. It was a short visit but a great one. It was so nice to connect with Lisa's family. I didn't have much time to connect with them when we were together last summer, so it was great getting to know them a little more.

It was time to get back on the road again. We travelled to Stansted, Québec. I wasn't sure how I would be received when I arrived. I had lived there with my great aunt Mary when I was 19 (and at that time, was expected to work at the local granite quarry) and had not been back since. As I pulled into the little town, I found the family home I stayed at quite easily. The village hadn't changed much; it was like going back in time.

It was great to catch up with Val and Kim, my cousins. It was nice to be welcomed by them; they saw a man to be proud of. I believe my great aunt Mary would be proud of who I am becoming and the direction I am going in, helping and coaching people. I was happy to have another great experience with my family.

To P.E.I.

Onward again to P.E.I., we made it in one day. It was great to see Lisa's mom again. She's so kind, welcoming, and fun to be with.

P.E.I was fantastic, and we had a great time. We celebrated Canada Day there in the little town of North Rustico. For me, it was one of the better Canada days. The fun-filled day was finished with fireworks over the water.

I did have an interesting experience just before the fireworks that I need to tell you about. Lisa had a hard time getting her dad up to dance to the music, and he didn't want to budge, so knowing how much I love Lisa and want the best for her, I marched over to her dad

Embracing the Warmth of the Sun, the Wind in My Hair, and the Blue Skies

and told him that he needed to get up to dance with his daughter and that in doing so, he would make her happy. Well, he got up with a little grumble on the side. However, I'm glad I stand up for the people I love.

During our one-week stay on the island, Lisa was busy promoting her book. We did a book launch at the senior's centre and at a few Indigo bookstores. I love supporting my wonderful wife, and I'm very proud of her.

Diabetes

When we got to P.E.I, my counts were really high, and I was worried a little. Like I say, life is a choice, and I can choose to make forward walking or backward walking choices. I had been eating unhealthy food, so it was time to buckle down and eat better and walk more. Within a week, I had my counts back down.

One of the biggest things I know today is that life is about choices and consequences. I know that the choices are all up to me, and I'm able to make great choices.

Lisa and I packed up the car after our time on P.E.I. and on our drive, we worked more on this book.

For the first time in my life, I felt like I belonged. I felt like I was making a difference and had a voice.

It felt great having conversations with Lisa about our future and making investments together. We discussed buying a property. A church! We thought we would buy it and put several units in it to rent out. It's an idea at this point.

My Perfect Storm

On our way back west, we had a minor problem with the car. It seemed to work its way out, though.

My shift

We stopped at Dean's again in Ottawa for a night. Again, it was great feeling like I belonged and had a voice. I felt a great shift inside of me. It was still a strange feeling, but it was getting more comfortable.

Kill Bear Park

At last, I returned to the spot where I had my very first memory that began this book. The one with my dad shouting, "I'm going to kill that little son of a bitch when I get my hands on him."

Well, Lisa and I arrived around 3 pm at Kill Bear Park and set up camp. Since I was only young, about eight years old, when I first stayed at Kill Bear, I actually didn't really remember much of what the park physically looked like.

We walked to the beach and marvelled at the beauty of Georgian Bay. I was feeling pretty happy and content.

Back at our site, I attempted to BBQ some steak, but the BBQ had different plans and didn't work. So, we had to pan-fry the steak, which isn't my favourite way to cook a steak, that's for sure, but it tasted good all the same.

After dinner, we went back down to the beach and the rocky shoreline to watch the sunset and enjoy the beauty around us.

Embracing the Warmth of the Sun, the Wind in My Hair, and the Blue Skies

Scott and Lisa enjoying the sunset at Kill Bear Park in Owen Sound, Ontario

There were other people and families around us enjoying the sunset, too. We chatted with them. It was fun watching their kids running around having fun.

At first, the sunset was bright and beautiful, but soon, the clouds didn't cooperate, so we didn't see much of a sunset.

The young boy of the family that was beside us started to cry loudly. At first, this annoyed me, but when I found out that the boy had shoved an acorn up his nose, I felt bad for him. His parents would probably have to take him to the hospital. I was feeling a sense of empathy and compassion, something kind of new to me.

We walked back to our site. I was thinking it would be great to get some of my family back together and to go to Kill Bear for a reunion. We could talk about some old stories and start that process of healing.

Fears

Writing this book has been a challenge. I had a fear of judgement. A fear of pain. A fear of how things were and knowing that I have moved past a lot of the pain of my past.

I've shared many vulnerable parts of my life in this story. I've learned to change the stories that are so ingrained in my thoughts and that I've been telling myself over and over my whole life. Thanks to Lisa, my friends, and my coaches, who have supported me in seeing myself differently so that I can choose how to show up in life.

Thank you for reading about my life and for coming on this journey of healing and growth. Thank you for providing the space I needed to share so I can let go, and thank you for being a witness in seeing that I can choose to move forward in my life. Anything is possible.

I look forward to your feedback. If you want to connect with me, come meet me and my wife, Lisa, at forwardwalkingchoices.com

THREE OFFERS WITH CALLS TO ACTION

Visit Forward Walking Choices Online Coaching at forwardwalkingchoices.com for one-to-one, couples, and small group coaching.

Book Scott Brearley for a one-hour online presentation on his book, his journey, and the experience and wisdom he has gained over 55 years. Visit forwardwalkingchoices.com to book.

Book Scott and Lisa Brearley for a two-hour online presentation on how we keep our relationship healthy, support each other in our journey of growth, and continue to move forward in our relationship.

SPEAKER BIO

Scott Brearley is a 56-year-old man with experiences that many would not have survived. He grew up in Burlington, Ontario, where he experienced a life of trauma, abuse, and addictions, all of which were exacerbated after a major life-threatening accident at the age of seven.

After moving to British Columbia, the dark cloud called life seemed to follow him. He experienced an unsuccessful marriage, cancer, diabetes, numerous motorcycle accidents, death, and even having to choose to keep many of his family members out of his life.

Scott found himself in a personal development program with the Personal Success Institute in 2018, which sparked a change. With many tools under his belt, from growing through the Alcoholics Anonymous program to making major decisions in his life, such as having a radical prostatectomy, Scott is choosing brighter days on the other side.

With an emphasis on moving forward in his life, Scott has persevered in his own personal growth journey through many more programs, beating cancer, controlling his diabetes through food, and earning his certification as a life coach.

Scott's trials and tribulations have shaped the person he is today: a strong, determined man on a mission to provide guidance to others through his coaching business.

Scott and his wife Lisa are teaming up together—a force to be reckoned with! Join them to hear about their journeys in life. Be inspired to see how they make their relationship work and what it takes to be fully committed and support each other in their growth and this life journey.